For full audio of this book
as read by the author (plus commentary) please visit:
www.mysilentteam.com/public/783.cfm

If you would like to begin receiving the most popular
Internet success newsletter in the world for **free** please visit:

www.SilentJim.com

We'd love to add you to our email subscriber list with no obligation!
Over 216,702 others have already joined!

Use Facebook?

We have a large community of online entrepreneurs and fans of this book who
hang out online together—I hope you'll join us! Here's the link:
www.facebook.com/groups/mysilentteam

TABLE OF CONTENTS

CHAPTER 1

What This Book Will Do For You

CAUTION: Reading this book just might make you certifiably unemployable! What I mean is, it could make you so eager and excited about the opportunities I'm about to show you that you could find it hard to be satisfied with any "real job."

For several years now my team and I have taught literally thousands of people how to "make the leap" and begin making a great income from home using the Internet creatively.

To be clear, I'm talking about doing something you believe in for a living—something you are proud of, love doing and can't wait to do each day. I want you to get all this, while earning the level of income you need to support a family. To get you there, I'm going to show you the same strategies I've used myself for over a decade to provide 100% of the income for my family. Better yet, these are the ideas thousands of others have also embraced on their journey towards financial independence.

If that's what you want, I want to help make it happen!

My Story

I made a pretty bad decision in 2002 and as a result I wound up getting fired from the last real job I've ever had, but if I hadn't messed up so badly *you would not be reading this book*.

At the time of my bad decision, my wife was eight months pregnant with our third child and I was the sole bread winner. We were (and remain) committed to her being able to stay home with our kids.

Leading up to my bad decision, our bank account had grown pretty thin and the pressure was definitely on me to pick up the slack.

A year before this time I had tried to get things going again by making a horizontal move to a competitor in my industry, but things weren't panning out very well in this new job. A few months into the new job our family income had gone down—not up like we'd expected it would with my new job.

I was a software sales rep, and while I'd been a top performer at my previous company, my sales results at the new company were average at best and I was getting burned out on the entire industry. I was afraid of being "on my own" though, without a stable corporate career to lean on. So I thought another *job* was my only choice.

However, I couldn't go look for another job because I hadn't yet "put in the time" to be marketable again so soon. The base pay was *great* at the new job, so a part of me inside definitely thought I would be nuts to put my new job at risk. I tried hard to stay serious and make it work, but I found it very hard to focus and motivate myself.

The truth is, the rebel entrepreneur in me was raging to get out! I knew I was meant for more!

In my state of "boredom" with my career I'd started playing around online with eBay in my spare time. I found it interesting and motivating. I felt creative and inspired when I was working online . . . and it was all starting to work for me.

> **NOTE:** This book *isn't* just about eBay . . . this is just important foundational information for you.

Quickly I discovered that a few hours of spare time spent working on my online business ideas was earning me a very nice side income and I wanted to ramp if up—and I did!

Then I got fired!?

No one wants to get fired, but there are points in life where the news hits harder than it would have otherwise. This was one of those times. Remember, my wife Andrea was 8 months pregnant, and if there's one time in life where having health insurance is a good thing—it's then!

Remember my bad decision from the start of this chapter? Here's what happened . . .

I shared (in confidence) with my friend Chris who happened to also be my boss, that I was struggling to stay motivated in a job I just didn't love. My numbers as a salesman were decent, but they needed improvement and we discussed it candidly. I confided in him that I might be a few months from looking at going out on my own and taking a shot at going full time online with my own business, but I promised him loyalty and good effort until such time arrived.

"If I were to go out on my own someday . . ." I asked him, "what would we put into motion in a few months to help transition my large territory smoothly and slowly to a new sales rep?" I was looking for support and encouragement and feeling out his reaction. I was also hoping the process I'd described would take months or longer to unfold.

If you missed it, that was my bad decision. Telling my friend (who was also my boss) the truth about how I felt about my career. It never occurred to me that what happened next was how it would all unfold.

The next day I was fired because Chris told his boss (the company VP) and they decided in about 30 seconds that I should be let go.

The day *after* being fired:

I didn't send out resumes. I didn't start calling my "connections" in the biz.

I was done.

No looking back.

I determined to become one of the greatest success stories of online marketing that the world had ever seen. There was no going back.

My wife was a wreck for a few days there, but she believed in me and encouraged me. I had married an amazing girl (as if I needed any more evidence of that).

That was the start of my online career and I believe my story can do something powerful inside of you as well if you'll let it.

This book *has* played a role in thousands of people's lives, as I'll soon prove.

I wrote the first version of the book you are now reading and sold about 10 copies of it to customers of mine in early 2002 (before I was fired). At that time I had very few readers to give me feedback and even fewer who put my ideas into practice. Back then this was a book mainly about eBay.

You are now reading the 8th major update and re-release of this book. This version has very little in common with the original because things have changed so much online and I've matured considerably in my approach to building serious businesses online.

Recently I hosted an event for the readers of this book in Orlando FL. Nearly everyone pictured here has read this book, and dozens of them have built incredible business based on these ideas. The event sold out quickly—over 350 attended to learn about the ideas you'll be reading here.

An estimated 250,000+ people have either paid for or received and read earlier versions of this book. Such a large number of people have succeeded applying the ideas I've taught in the various versions of this book that I've become labeled as one of, if not *the* "most trusted" Internet marketer online for several years now as of this writing. It's a label I hold in the highest regard!

DO THIS: I've received many testimonials and success stories from my past customers and readers and posted them on a few of my sites. To get an idea of what others have to say about this book (past versions and this version) please visit these two pages:

http://www.jimcockrum.com/blog/success-stories
http://www.silentsalesmachine.com/testimonials

Many of the people behind the success stories are gathered at my two membership sites MySilentTeam.com and OfflineBiz.com. Hundreds of members log onto those sites daily and we've had thousands of members join since each of the sites launched. I'll talk more about those two sites and how they are different from each other later in the book.

> **DO THIS:** This book is about *what works* online as are my newsletter and membership sites found at OfflineBiz.com and MySilentTeam.com.

> I teach people how to establish multiple sources of *legitimate* automated online income by building businesses that will last and that they can be proud of—all without having to learn any technical skills.

I hope none of this comes across like I'm bragging, but I want to establish my credibility quickly so that you can relax knowing where I came from, who I am and why I'm qualified to teach you what I'm about to show you.

If you are ready to get serious about using the Internet the *right way* as a tool of influence and income, then I'm someone you should definitely be listening to.

> **TIP:** While some online "experts" are continually coming out with new products and selling them to the same audience over and over again, I've chosen to keep updating this one eBook over and over again and each time I pass it out to all my past customers at *no charge* while charging new customers very little to get a copy. I'm doing my best to raise the standard in my industry and raise your expectations of all "Internet Marketing experts."

Since 2002 my Internet marketing career has been rocketing upward—each year far surpassing the previous. I won't go into full detail here about my current situation because that information would be obsolete by the time you read this, but I can sum it up by saying "my stock has never been higher."

Thanks to the Internet and the implementation of the very ideas contained in this book I left my last full-time corporate job behind in 2002 and have since been able to work from home with my wife and five kids nearby. We travel, we've adopted three times internationally (twice since being fired), we support the causes we believe in, we volunteer, and my kids have the best private tutors they could ever have schooling them in our own home—their mom and I.

There is no traditional job that can possibly lure me out of this lifestyle. I work the hours I want, work out and run 6 days per week (currently training to qualify for the Boston Marathon). I take the day off for a movie or museum with my kids whenever I get the urge to do so, and I earn way more than anyone I know with any traditional "job."

If you have a similar goal to quit your job and work the Internet part-time while pulling in a full-time income then my goal is that this book will be the first steps in getting you there.

Another important note

I've incorporated several ideas into this book from my first ever best selling "real" book about using the Internet as a creative marketing tool. That hardcover book was written in 2011 for Wiley Publishing (the 'For Dummies' publishers), but nearly all of the lessons are timeless and not short term trends. You can get details on that book at 101FreeMarketing.com. That "101 Free Marketing" book was ranked as the #1 top selling Internet Marketing book on Amazon.com for several weeks after launch . . . and was one of the top selling books in the world for several days after launch as well! If you like this book, please check that book out too and leave a review for it on Amazon—I'd sure appreciate it.

TESTIMONY: From a reader of the 101FreeMarketing.com book:

You produce the best quality content on marketing. I've read so many business books this year and I'd say yours (101FreeMarketing.com) gave the most immediately actionable info that didn't cost me a bombshell.

Regards,

—H. Katsonga, Woodward, London UK

Read dozens more reader comments on Amazon.com. Just search for "Free Marketing Jim Cockrum" and you'll see the book.

While there is perhaps a 10% overlap between the 101FreeMarketing.com book and this one, this book differs because the goal of this book is to help you *discover*, *start* and grow multiple income streams by choosing from among the three proven business models I'll be showing you. This book will help you establish *hands free income online*, while the

101FreeMarketing.com book is about online and offline marketing for any established business and *does not* offer up specific business models.

> **A BIT OF HISTORY:** Silent Sales Machine has sold well for over a decade and was priced as high as $50 in the past.

What do I hope this book does for you?

Like so many others before you, I hope you'll find new streams of income for you and your family. I hope you'll find more free time and less stress to go along with the new income. I love seeing parents get to stay home—my heart especially goes out to dads. I love bringing dads home. I love helping leaders use the Internet in creative ways to spread their message. From the bottom of my heart I want to help you succeed!

> **DO THIS:** While updating this chapter I got a great message from a student who just went full time with her Internet business & quit her corporate career!
>
> Here's a 45 second video that shows you what she posted on Facebook and the huge reaction of your fellow readers of this book:
>
> http://youtu.be/Ni4Rlt5vH88

Perhaps the first goal of this book is to get you to look at the opportunities that the Internet has to offer with realistic excitement. I'll show you what works and even some common misconceptions being spread by "experts" who should know better. I should know because I've been successfully teaching what works since 2002 with plenty of proof to back up my theories (over 1,000 success stories!)

A "Silent Sales Machine" idea strikes . . .

I'll tell you what a "Silent Sales Machine" is very soon, but first a bit more about my early success and how you can apply the same ideas to your online adventure:

The idea for my first "Silent Sales Machine" hit me like a ton of bricks one day. I even remember the exact spot where I was while driving down the road when it hit me. I nearly had to pull over because I knew I had just had a *huge* idea. I finally realized the amazing power of the Internet as a 24/7 tool for connecting with prospects, customers, partners, etc.

That one idea I had several years ago changed my life and the lifestyle my family enjoys to this day and I think you are in for some eye-opening moments very soon as well as you read on.

My realization was this:

I was going to stop trying to "drive traffic," stop trying to search out customers, and instead focus on finding creative ways to engage with customers where they were already gathered—in like minded groups. That idea and several other foundational concepts I have for you will make more sense as you read further into this book.

> **A CHALLENGE FOR YOU:** Convince yourself that creative income that *does not* require tedious daily effort *is possible* online. *You can achieve it* as so many others have already done by using a

little effort and a proven system. Do not proceed until you are *convinced*. Need evidence? Visit my blog at JimCockrum.com, MySilentTeam.com or OfflineBiz.com or any of my other sites and check out the numerous testimonials and success stories.

A note about the "clickable" links in this book

You will notice that there are many links in this book to help you go quickly to a website that further helps illustrate a lesson or an example. Many of these links are "redirect" links that point to my website "MySilentTeam.com/XXXX" where "XXXX" is the redirect portion of the link. If this confuses you don't worry—it will make sense as you read along. I've taken the "redirect" approach so that I can easily update links that are outdated. If you happened to encounter an outdated link please let us know and we'll fix it for you. There is contact information on the download page for this book here:

http://www.mysilentteam.com/public/783.cfm

Part of the beauty of eBooks is that they are "living" documents that can be updated and corrected on the fly by the author. Let's take advantage of that—help me keep it as accurate as possible for everyone until the next update (which you'll get for free as a buyer of any previous version of this book!)

Concluding thoughts for Chapter 1

I wrote this book for you. It contains my best ideas and is my best effort to help you achieve your dreams online. I give this book to family and friends and now to you. I get emails and messages almost daily from people who have been inspired to success with the simple yet profoundly effective concepts in this book. I'll equip you with some great ideas and the tools and training to get you there. Hold on for a great ride!

I look forward to hearing your feedback!

—Jim Cockrum

JimCockrum.com

CHAPTER 2

What are Silent Sales Machines?

If you haven't figured it out yet . . .

A "Silent Sales Machine" is the name I've given to my online income streams. Each stream of income is a quiet smooth running machine that churns out sales and profits 100% on autopilot (or nearly 100% autopilot).

In some cases I'm selling physical products on eBay, Amazon, or from a website, and in other cases the "product" is digital. A "digital" product is an audio, video, or downloadable eBook. I also run membership sites, discussion forums and have large email lists. All of these business models produce income and I'm going to show you how to do what I do.

The power of residual income

The "Silent Sales Machine" techniques that I am going to show you will allow you to set up multiple "hands-free" income streams by harnessing the power of the Internet. Even if it takes a little effort to get the first machine established, you will be well rewarded for your efforts! I set up my first "Silent Sales Machine" in less than a week from start to finish. Once established, it began making steady income for me while my time was free to create more income streams.

> **NOTE:** This reader made a YouTube video about how he went from zero income streams to 9 very quickly using the ideas in this book:
>
> http://youtu.be/FKRw-rcEIWE

Today I have about 35 income streams—none of which require daily attention. Sure, some streams dry up and others require a bit of work to maintain, but in the end, I'm not reliant on any one stream as it runs silently and predictably into my bank account.

Some of my income streams are as small as $100-$200 per month. Some streams are significantly larger. Add them all up and I'd have to work 60 hour weeks as the CEO of a major corporation to get the same income results—and I wouldn't get to be home with my family during the day or enjoy the flexible lifestyle we've become so accustomed to since 2002.

I *rarely* trade dollars for hours any more. I'm even frequently approached by traditional businesses that want to work with me on projects. I typically scare them away by charging upwards of $750 per hour, but even when someone is smart enough to pay me that much per hour (I'm more than worth it), I still often feel like I'm selling myself short because I'm trading "dollars" for my most valuable asset . . . "hours."

One of the most popular blog posts I've ever written got literally *hundreds* of replies when I posted it. It was on this very topic of automated income. Here's the simple question I posed—it's a choice between two income opportunities:

Imagine you are given a choice between two options:

OPTION ONE: You can have *four* separate 100% *automated* income streams that each produce $1K per month consistently. (Total $4k/month) with minimal or *no* work involved in keeping them flowing

OPTION TWO: You can have *one* income stream that requires a few hours of daily attention and produces $6K or more per month. (Total $6K/month)

What's your choice?

Hundreds of readers of this book have answered this simple question in the last few years. Check out their responses, or leave an answer yourself here:

http://www.jimcockrum.com/blog/?p=178

Click on the "comments" button on that blog post to join the conversation.

I'm hoping you see the value in option one above. It shows me that you understand how valuable your greatest asset is. *Time*.

The Internet has been the foundation for all of this for me. I'm happy to share the story with you now of how I help people turn hobbies, passions and interests into online income and also how I help them create multiple income streams.

As with any successful business, work is required in launching it, and at least occasional maintenance and attention is needed no matter how "automated" you make it, but the Internet is a unique tool that allows anyone to create multiple income streams or "Silent Sales Machines."

If the income is tied to your hobby or passion it may be something you work at every day, and that's fine, but I'll be showing you how to automate to the greatest degree possible so that you only work when and how you want to work. Do only the things you love to do. That's the goal. Here's an example of a success story from one of my students to illustrate:

> **TESTIMONY:** I gotta give you credit for my story, Jim. You are the one who showed me eBay and how to harness it by driving traffic to my site. My efforts have now spurred a great cult following of my business. My thanks to you.
>
> My story:
>
> I use to be an indie filmmaker, it was my dream since I was a small kid that I wanted to see my work up on the big screen. I wrote, directed, edited, and produced 10 films all on my own. I did them all on my own because I just did not have the $$ to hire people, so I made them dirt cheap.

I got into the Tribeca Film Festival, won numerous awards, and even had a feature action film go international. All was great! But there was no income really, I worked odd jobs to make a buck. Late twenties hit and I said I needed to make some money. I couldn't keep bumming off my folks. But I did not want to work for anyone else either. I knew I had the talents and the skills to do my own thing.

My idea:

All through my college and filmmaking years I had a classic VW, but I knew nothing about other cars. I only knew the bug. I am an artist so ya gotta have a bug. I grabbed a 1968 Beetle rotted to hell for $350.00 and I wanted to restore it. My father thought I was crazy but we did it together. I knew nothing about restoring cars, my dad had some mechanical skills when he was young working in a Brooklyn garage, but we had never worked on a VW.

Thanks to the Internet, there are many resources to learn any craft you want. If you have the drive and a desire to do something great and be independent, there's never been a better time to be alive than now!

I learned these skills from you Mr. Cockrum, and sold that Bugger on eBay motors! We made food money on it! My father and I looked at each other and said, "We gotta get into this!" So from a one car garage to now a 2000 sq ft facility, we are kicking butt! We developed a nice track record on eBay and we are now taking orders for my "Build-A-Bug" program. We are running our business with a year and a half wait time. People want us to build a Bug just for them!

What made me stand out from the crowd is that I filmed my Bugs. No one is doing what I am doing when it comes to selling on eBay motors. All bidders are exposed to over 50 pics of my cars and full HD video.

I also do 'How To' Tips on Beetle restoration thrown up on YouTube (my ID on YouTube.com is brighteyefilms), that led me to sell a full two hour DVD on Headliner installation, (I sell the DVD's via drop shipping one at a time using Kunaki.com like you showed me). I answer two hours of fan mail in the morning and two hours at night just for the Bug biz.

Sorry this is so long winded, but my example shows if you have a passion to be successful with a product you love, you can do it.

Every resource is available out there for you. I am always learning and staying up to date with the trends, this will give you the edge and make you stand out from your competition.

—Chris Vallone
  ClassicVWbugs.com

Notice how he's leading a "tribe" (to borrow a term from Seth Godin). Notice how he's growing an audience of like minded people and then giving them what they want. I'll share more success stories like these throughout the book.

More about the story of my first "Silent Sales Machine"

For me it all started on eBay—but it didn't stop there as you'll soon see!

Before I launched my first "Silent Sales Machine" I was selling a handful of items at a time on eBay and making a decent side income doing it.

This was not "autopilot" income. eBay was (and still is in most cases) a lot of hard work.

Then everything changed . . .

One day I took a hard look at the "hit counter" for my auctions. A "hit counter" tells you how many visitors you are getting. I had *hundreds* and even *thousands* of people in some cases looking at each of my auctions. Very few of those hundreds of shoppers were sending me any money though. There was only one winner/buyer per auction.

I also knew that *everyone* on the Internet was talking about trying to get "targeted traffic" to their websites. Traffic is the same as "visitors." We've all heard the saying that a beautiful website is useless without targeted traffic, right?

That's when it occurred to me. There are countless websites that would kill for some traffic like I was getting on eBay if there was a way to push some of the traffic over to their website! There I was on eBay getting a lot of traffic, but I was ignoring virtually every visitor except for the one visitor who was my winning bidder.

I set out to tap into the *huge* volume of traffic on eBay and funnel it to other places off eBay *without violating eBay policy*.

Once I figured it out, my business *took off fast*!

By listing a single item on eBay I was growing my audience and increasing my sales *even if* the item I was selling sold for a total loss.

I began growing my email mailing list, making repeat sales and more importantly earning hands free income from all that eBay traffic.

That was my first "Silent Sales Machine" . . . now I have many "machines" running, and very few of them are reliant on eBay.

> **MILLION DOLLAR TIP:** Adjust your thinking about "Investing in an online business."
>
> Success on the Internet is rarely if ever about making a large upfront investment into new uncharted waters. It's rarely if ever about starting with a big beautiful website and then desperately chasing down traffic and customer.
>
> Nearly all of the successful Internet entrepreneurs that I know are simply using inexpensive tools and slightly creative strategies to get a piece of already proven, popular markets. Next they automate . . . and repeat the process.

Concluding thoughts for Chapter 2

Earning income from multiple online sources is possible. I'm going to show you where to start and where not to start right in this book.

A word of caution:

Even though this is a book about multiple income streams don't make the mistake of thinking that you can launch multiple successful businesses all at once. Especially as you are getting started, each smooth flowing income stream will require a period of intense focused effort and attention in order to launch and establish the income stream. Once established, each income stream can then be automated to whatever degree possible to free up your time for more streams. Do you remember the children's story about the racing tortoise and hare? The lesson from the book holds true online as well. Slow and steady wins the race.

> **TIP:** Want some tips for keeping your priorities straight while growing multiple online businesses? Here's a blog post about that exact topic:
>
> http://www.jimcockrum.com/blog/?p=2786
>
> You also might enjoy this article titled, "How I manage multiple businesses and a large family":
>
> http://www.jimcockrum.com/blog/?p=2726
>
> I've learned a lot about keeping priorities straight in the last decade. There are some good tips in those articles.

CHAPTER 3

The Tools and Basic Skills of Online Success

There are a few paths to predictable success online that nearly anyone can get into with little or no investment. The only requirement is some focused, determined effort.

I often say that *no new skills* are required in order to succeed online, and while I stand by that statement, there are a few basic tools and "minor skills" that will really lay down a nice foundation for you to grow from. Once you grasp these basics, you can be successful in countless ways online.

Once you have the basic tools and skills in place there are *three categories of opportunities* that will open up to you. I call them the "CES" models.

That's my "CES" model of success. C = Consult, E = Expand, and S = Sell Stuff.

1. C = Consult. Help other business owners apply basic Internet Marketing skills to their business and prosper from your efforts in helping them succeed.

2. E = Expand. Find a profitable niche market, be a leader in that niche and give your followers fantastic content while also selling them products, services, training, or information that is of interest to them.

3. S = Sell Stuff. Sell profitable physical goods through your own site, Amazon or eBay and find creative ways to automate the entire system and grow a huge customer following for future sales.

I've been doing all three of these business models online for over a decade and have taught thousands of others how to do one or all of them as well through my coaching and my two membership sites (MySilentTeam.com & OfflineBiz.com). While you certainly don't have to do all three (we have thousands of students doing only one of the three), I've found that the three biz models do blend together and compliment each other quite nicely as you add each new stream.

> **NOTE:** Here's a quick look at a blog post I wrote that breaks down my multiple income streams in a pie-chart:
>
> http://www.jimcockrum.com/blog/?p=2768

The rest of this book will equip you for success in one or all three of these models and will also identify multiple related businesses that might be of interest to you, but before we go too far down that path let's talk about the basic skills and tools you'll need no matter what direction you take.

3.1 Igniting Email Marketing

This is the longest segment in the book for good reason. I love email marketing and no matter what you've heard to the contrary, it's still an incredible way to connect with new prospects and stay in touch with your audience.

The *number one* asset of nearly *all* big time success stories online is this . . .

They have a *big* email list that they can go to over and over again for predictable results.

A FEW EMAIL SUCCESS STORIES:

Just in case you are thinking that "email is dead" here's proof that it's alive and well! I recently held my first ever live conference. I announced it to my email list and it sold out quickly—so much so that we had to turn people away. That's the picture of the crowd that you saw at the start of this book.

Also, when I launched my first "real book" into bookstores around the world, it shot to the #1 position on Amazon in the "Marketing" and "Internet Marketing" categories using *only* email marketing. I didn't spend a *dime* on *any* other marketing efforts. Here's a short video with detailed proof of the success of that book launch:

http://www.youtube.com/watch?v=roqH5KaCYUM

Here's another video that shows how I made over $7,000 in a day by sending an attractive offer to my email list:

http://www.youtube.com/watch?v=AleIiiMEg1g

That sort of thing happens *all the time* . . . it's all thanks to email.

Email marketing is widely considered to be the most powerful form of marketing in use today. When done right the ROI is 50:1 or more. Most months my own personal ROI is *far higher* than that. This means for every $1 I spend growing and managing my mailing list I can expect to put at least $50 in the bank. There's even better news though. Most of the activities I do in an effort to grow my email list cost me nothing except a little bit of time. And they are perpetual—meaning they keep on working indefinitely (i.e. setting up a YouTube video to attract subscribers).

If you learn *only* one new skill related to success online it should be email management in my opinion. Nearly all other technical aspects of your success online can be easily "crowd sourced" or outsourced, but you *must* have a "grow the list" mentality.

> **TIP:** Where do I go to find skilled workers for nearly all other aspects of my business outside of email marketing?

Sites like Fiverr.com, oDesk.com, vWorker.com and Elance.com are all places where you can find a worker to outsource nearly any online project. When I post a quick question on Twitter or Facebook and allow the "crowd" to help me out with an issue I also consider that "crowd sourcing." In other words, there's no need to start reading a bunch of books about graphics, programming and web design in order to be successful on the Internet.

Learning the possibilities and automation strategies behind email marketing is something too important to leave in the hands of anyone else until you grasp it yourself. It's also extremely inexpensive to learn and manage.

I'll restate this business fact a different way to make it timeless and across the board relevant:

> There is no asset more powerful in *any* business than a list of customers who have "signed up" indicating that they want to hear from you. Having as much contact information as possible makes the list even more powerful. Currently the *most profitable*, *cheapest* and *easiest* way to stay in touch with and grow a relationship with such a list is unquestionably via mass email marketing.

Still, I understand the intimidation . . .

Take this frequently asked question for example (I get variations of this question often):

"Jim, I'm not much of a writer and I don't see myself ever writing an email newsletter, but I've started growing my mailing list and now I don't know what to do with my list. I only have about 200 people on my list so far and I feel like I need to do *something* with it, but I can't do a newsletter for that small of a list, can I? I don't even like to write! I'm not all that passionate about my niche market and I'm not sure I have much to offer my list really. What should I do?"

In this section we'll address all the issues I've raised so far and a few others you probably haven't considered yet regarding the use of email as a business power tool (for *any* business).

You need to be growing a mailing list and turning those email leads into lifetime customers and none of the excuses I mentioned so far (or the big list of excuses I'm going to show you below) are relevant—nor are they nearly as big of a stumbling block as some people make them out to be.

In fact, *one tool* resolves all these issues. This *one tool* that I'm about to tell you about is *by far* the *most important tool* in my online business. If I had 30 seconds to give you a million dollar piece of advice, it would include telling you about this *one tool*.

DO THIS: I frequently tell people to stop building their skill set on the Internet. Stop learning PHP, HTML, Java, graphics design, and all that other techie geeky stuff. The winners on the Internet are not the techie geeks. The winners are those who *take action* and outsource all the geeky stuff to geeky people who like doing it. *But* . . . there is *one tool* you need to learn and understand . . .

I wrote a popular blog article recently about my observations about the power of email marketing. If you aren't convinced yet maybe this will help:

http://www.jimcockrum.com/blog/?p=748

So, what is this amazing tool you should have?

The tool you need to understand is an email autoresponder. My personal favorite currently is AWeber (Click this link to check it out: http://jimcockrum.aweber.com).

You can learn a *ton* about the power of autoresponders and bulk email management from AWeber.

I pay AWeber about $100 per month to manage several very large email lists. If you are new to AWeber, your costs will be lower because you only pay higher fees as your list grows.

AWeber is my favorite bill to pay every month because my ROI hovers around 500+:1 (for every dollar spent, I easily earn back $500). It's economical and it completely automates the process of adding new subscribers to my various lists, keeping me compliant with spam issues, allowing subscribers to change their contact details, automating the transition of "prospects" into "customers" for appropriate messaging and allowing them to easily remove themselves when they want to get off my list. The number of automated and profitable features is astounding!

I'll go deeper into the "automation" features of AWeber later in this chapter.

To be clear, the *one tool* that will be the most vital to your success no matter what direction your online business goes is *email automation*.

TIP: Here's a video that shows you how I manage over 100 email lists virtually hands free using AWeber.com:

http://youtu.be/z7JSFPc3m80

Let's kill some "email" excuses . . .

Here are some common excuses I hear as reasons for not getting into email marketing. See if any of these sound like you. I offer a short rebuttal for each one and will go deeper on each point throughout this chapter:

EXCUSE: I'm not a great writer.

Don't write long messages. Pretend it's an email to a friend. Keep it under five lines except in unusual circumstances.

EXCUSE: But I don't have anything to sell in each message.

You don't have to sell every time—nor should you try to. Give your loyal subscribers great free information and advice. Link to good blog articles or current events of interest. Build trust. Provide value. A loyal list is a list of people who will buy from you now *and* later. You can simply include your business phone number and remind them you are there if they need anything . . . a nice personal touch.

EXCUSE: But where will I find good content for my messages?

That is *lame, lame, lame*! Have you heard of Google.com? Start there, or go buy five of the best sellers on your topic from Amazon.com and condense the points they make into brief tips.

Need more ideas? Find an expert who *is* passionate about your niche and promote their products (for a percentage) and use *their* sales copy (with permission of course). Perhaps you could interview a top sales rep in your field and find out what customers want. Remember, build a relationship, establish your expertise, and give subscribers *great* information. They will buy eventually, but it costs you nothing if they don't because email is virtually free.

EXCUSE: But what if my list is a combination of people with different niche interests?

You need to separate your subscribers and put them in groups with similar interests. AWeber allows you to have as many lists as you'd like. You can easily send out a combined "broadcast" to as many of your lists as you'd like, but when in doubt, create a new list and separate out your subscribers as much as possible. I have about 60 lists on AWeber and it's no harder to manage than if I had only one.

EXCUSE: But what about the spam issue? Don't only spammers use email to sell online?

One of the important issues to keep in mind as you start growing your mailing list is the spam issue. Don't be intimidated though. It's easy to stay 100% legit if you use a confirmed opt-in (sometimes called *double opt-in*) strategy for all subscribers. AWeber allows you to automate this easily. There is more on this topic below as well. I'm coaching every kind of business on proper email use and it's a powerful strategy used by all kinds of businesses and even churches to mass market their message in an easy and cost effective way. Email simply works and it's a 100% legit way to market your ideas too.

EXCUSE: But how will I manage all those subscribers? I don't want multiple lists with hundreds or thousands of names to worry about.

AWeber makes it simple. I manage my list that has seen over 250,000 people subscribe, cancel, change addresses, move from list to list, etc. for *far* less effort than I manage my own personal email account! I'm talking about a few minutes of effort monthly to put together any mailings that I want to do. All the rest of the "work" on my email management is on 100% autopilot.

EXCUSE: But what if a customer wants to get off my list or change their name or email address etc.? That sounds like a lot of work.

That is all automated. There is automatically a link placed at the bottom of all emails sent out that allows customers to manage their own account. When we get a request asking us to do these things, we refer customers back to the link at the bottom of the email they got from us.

But isn't email dying?

For several years now there have been rumors that email is "going away." I think it was the spam issue that got everyone so worked up initially, and then it was the sheer volume that was supposedly going to overwhelm us and "turn us off," and then Facebook rumors started swirling etc.

> **TIP:** Don't make the mistake of thinking that Social Media is replacing email as the more effective marketing tool! Check out the facts:
>
> http://www.jimcockrum.com/blog/?p=2696
>
> I contend that the *best* use of any influence you gain on social media should be used to *grow your email list*!

My perspective is that email marketing will continue to be where serious conversations and interactions between friends and businesses take place for a long time. Here are some thoughts on the issue:

Spam is coming under control. It's not that there are fewer spammers, but technology is staying ahead of them, and the "law" keeps nailing them. Email service providers are getting smarter too. More spam is blocked now than ever, and the ratio of "good email" getting through is higher than ever for just about every email marketer who I talk to. I love my Gmail.com account. I'd say it's 98% accurate on identifying spammers and when it accidentally calls good email "spam," I fix it with a click and it never happens again with that sender.

I'd venture to guess I get way more email than you probably do, but with a bit of organizing effort I stay on top of it quite easily. That's a whole different topic of course, but if a busy guy with multiple businesses to run can stay on top of his email "easily"—so can everyone else. My point is, email isn't overwhelming to most of us—instead it's a vital communication tool that is here longterm.

Even if/when we all start to shift away from email someday, you will easily be able to transition if you have a large email list because the cost of communicating to your entire list is so inexpensive. Just tell the members of your list where else they can find you. Note: Facebook and Twitter *are not* a replacement for email now, nor are they likely ever to be.

You need only to ensure that people *want* to hear from you and you won't have any trouble. Of course it also makes sense to have other contact info on your prospects and clients. Get as much of it as you can right down to their second address and fax number if you want to, but email is the least expensive and most effective business marketing tool that has ever been used by man, so ignore it at your own peril.

Cutting edge companies like Google continue to pour millions into expanding and managing their own email tools and services that they use themselves, and supply to millions of users worldwide. Google is "sold" on the long term benefits of email as a serious tool for marketing. By the way . . . Gmail is by far my favorite email tool and it's free!

Which is better, a website or an email list? Shouldn't I just focus on getting traffic to my website?

There are a couple of reasons why having an email list is clearly better than a website in almost all cases.

Visitors to a website can click away at any moment—not so with an email list! If your content is relevant and useful, your subscribers will read it! Even if your subscribers have an old slow Internet connection, they still get email, and they can print out and read your newsletter at their leisure.

You are also building a relationship over time with your readers. This will lead to sales opportunities you haven't even imagined yet.

Products will come and go. Major websites and trends will come and go. A loyal email list of prospects who are willing to read your messages and consider buying products you create or endorse is a long term profit engine that is relatively easy to maintain and will never disappear. This is the ultimate "Silent Sales Machine."

Hopefully we've now killed off your excuses regarding using email marketing as a serious business tool!

Some basic terms of email marketing

Below are a few basic terms (in logical order, not alphabetized) that you'll need to understand in order to effectively "speak the language" of an email marketer:

Subscriber: A subscriber is an individual who has expressed an interest in receiving email from you. Treat your subscribers like people, not like random email addresses. Even as your email list grows, you should always write your email messages as if you were writing them to one person. A subscriber is a valuable prospect, customer, or partner who has entered into a sacred trust with you allowing you to interrupt their day with a message whenever you have something of value to share. That privilege can and will be easily revoked at any point when you've stopped earning the right.

Email list: Any business or customer who I've ever worked with has required at least a handful of lists in order to manage their business properly. Your prospects can go on one list, while customers belong on a separate list. Your top customers should all go on their own list as well. Those are just some examples of different lists that you might have within your one email management account. The movement of individuals from one list to another can be automated as well. For example an online purchase of any kind could trigger a move that lifts an email address from the prospect list and onto to the customer list. You can't just put everyone on to one big list and expect to stay relevant. You'll need to segment your lists in as many creative ways as possible in order to be as effective as possible. Don't be intimidated by this process. I have over 60 lists of my own and the segmentation of those lists is on 100% autopilot through my email management service. This is why I suggest you use a good email management service, and also learn the basics of email management.

Spam: Spam is a loosely defined term that is used for any unwanted email that appears in an end user's email box. In my opinion there are two kinds of spam. One of them is a serious matter (easily avoided), and the other less serious type of spam needs to be managed, but isn't a serious threat to you or your business in any way.

Serious spam: Serious spam is generated when someone legally or illegally gathers a bunch of email addresses by purchasing them, scraping the Internet for them, entering them into a computer from a handwritten list, or by any other questionable means. Even sending relevant messages to such a list of emails is potentially considered a serious spam violation and is cause for some concern (or great concern if you "scraped" or bought the addresses). Using a legitimate email delivery service such as AWeber.com, GetResponse.com, iContact.com, MailChimp.com or ConstantContact.com will virtually ensure that you never violate such serious spam boundaries. This assurance comes from the fact that these email services have built in safeguards that do not allow spamming activity to occur via their email management service, so you can never accidentally engage in sending spam even if you are acting in ignorance and innocence.

"Not so serious" spam: "Not so serious" spam happens occasionally to *anyone* with a significantly sized email list. It happens when a fully confirmed subscriber loses interest in your message, forgets who you are, disagrees with your message, or even accidentally clicks the spam button in their email control panel. This happens to small and large email marketers alike and it *will* happen to you. If a significant percentage of your subscribers all accuse you of spam simultaneously, then you could have some trouble, but typically only a tiny fraction of any given email broadcast will result in spam complaints assuming you are handling your email broadcast activities correctly. With over 100,000 subscribers on my lists I get accused of "spam" in a "not so serious" way almost daily. As long as fewer than one in one thousand people cry "spam" when my email broadcasts go out, then I don't worry and neither does anyone else. Typically with an email blast to my 100,000 prospects I can easily expect around 30-40 spam complaints. No one cares about this low percentage of complaints. Unless more than .01% of my subscribers are crying spam at the same time, there is no issue. My email management service tracks it all for me and they let me know when I'm pushing the limit on any given message so I can avoid the same mistake twice on my message, or approach (frequency of email, topic being covered, length of email, etc. are all factors that can upset a subscriber).

Follow up sequence: (Sometimes called a "drip campaign.") Each new subscriber who you add to any of your email lists should receive an immediate response back from you (automated of course) confirming that they've been added to your list. This message should also contain relevant content that lets the subscriber know that they did the right thing in joining your list. After this initial message is delivered, an automatic and preset series of additional messages can then be delivered over time (days, weeks, months or more if appropriate). These additional messages are called the follow-up sequence. The follow-up sequence of emails that any new subscriber receives are vital to your email marketing success because it allows you to slowly build a trusting relationship with each new subscriber virtually on autopilot.

Broadcast: Even as your email list grows on autopilot you will have occasions where you want to send time sensitive information to the entire list. Maybe you're holding a special sale, or an important event is coming up on the calendar that they all need to know about. This type of one time "email blast" is called a broadcast. I broadcast a weekly newsletter to several of the lists that I manage. My email management service automatically ensures that even those subscribers who are subscribed on more than one of my lists each only get one copy of my newsletter when I send a broadcast to multiple lists. For example, if a "top customer" is on my "top customer" list as well as my "general customer" list they'll only get one copy of my newsletter in their inbox. This "list scrubbing" feature is a pretty standard feature of email management tools.

Opt-In: Any legitimate email marketer deals only with opt-in subscribers. I (along with most other marketers I know) take it a step further and only accept "confirmed" opt-in leads.

An opt-in lead is someone who has expressed an interest in joining your mailing list by signing up for your list. Many marketers consider this initial expression of interest to be enough of a confirmation to begin sending the new subscriber the content they've requested. The risk you take if you don't confirm each subscriber is that a third party could send you a bunch of "junk leads" and you would have no way to know if you were spamming the leads or not. Typos also occur frequently when subscribers fill out a form, and that can lead to spam.

To avoid any complications with spam laws I suggest you use *confirmed* opt-in only. Confirmed opt-in is the process where you automatically respond to an initial subscription request with a confirmation email. Unless the prospect takes the action requested in the confirmation email, they will receive no further communication from you. This will mean fewer subscribers ultimately, but you will avoid entirely any email address misspells, or a mean competitors trying to get you into "spam" trouble by adding a bunch of bad addresses to your list. My list of over 100,000 subscribers has been built using confirmed opt-in so I have virtually *no* spam worries. The only way I could be accused of spamming is if I go way off of message in my communications to my list. For example, if I have an email list about "pig farming" and I start sending them "parenting tips" I'll likely get a bunch of spam complaints.

Opt-out: One of the regulations that all email marketers must follow is to provide a way for your subscribers to easily opt out of receiving any further messages from you. This clickable link must be visibly present inside of each message that goes out. Rules like this compel me to convince you to allow a third-party service such as the ones I've mentioned to manage your email lists and mailings for you. Any reputable email management service will automatically insert an unsubscribe link at the bottom of every message that you send out.

Web Form: A web form is also sometimes called an opt-in form. It's simply the data form that a potential subscriber will use to join your mailing list. You could ask for just an email address on your web form, or require much more information (name, etc.). The less you ask for, the better your opt-in rate will be though. For example, I have a "squeeze page" at SilentJim.com that contains a basic web form for gathering email addresses for my newsletter. I ask simply for a name and email address. Most people just give me a first name instead of a full name, but that's all I need and the site converts quite well as a list building tool.

There are a few other terms and concepts to be aware of, but I don't want to overwhelm you. Armed only with the above list of terms you now understand the basics of email marketing and are more than ready to jump into the game.

Putting email to work

I've dedicated a significant portion of this section so far to convincing you that email marketing is a vital part of any business or organization's marketing efforts because of how inexpensive and highly effective it is. The biggest mistake you could make in pursuing email marketing as a strategy is to make it a manual process. The basic skills and tools of automating your email efforts are vital if you are to get the full benefit of your email marketing efforts.

Automating Your email Efforts

Once you understand the basics of email marketing you can begin to easily follow up with customers and prospects automatically. Like I mentioned before, I manage multiple email lists in my business on complete autopilot. On any given day we have hundreds of different subscribers joining different lists and even moving automatically from one list (prospect list) to other lists (customer list) seamlessly.

I won't go very far into the semi-technical details of setting all of this up because that information can easily be found on any reputable email management service for free. The services that come to mind are AWeber, GetResponse, MailChimp, ConstantContact, etc. Instead, I'll focus more on some lessons that I've learned about following up with my customers and prospects using email.

No matter how small your business is, you should use email in as automated a way as possible. For example, the vacation settings in a free Gmail account can be used to instantly reply to every customer that sends you an email. The reply email could have a link to a special offer or a blog site with additional information. That is about as simple as email automation gets, and it's not going to be very effective long term, but it's better than nothing. Of course you'll still reply to each customer with a personal message after they get the auto-reply. You will quickly outgrow this type of 'auto response' however.

> **TESTIMONY:** When I read Silent Sales Machine by Jim Cockrum, I was literally blown away. I did not sleep for 3 days because I knew this information would change my life—and it did.
>
> One of the premises of the book is:
>
> - Grow an audience (with an email list)
>
> - Give away valuable information
>
> - Develop a positive relationship with the readers
>
> - Occasionally mention products that YOU believe in and "sell stuff."
>
> - Use email marketing to automate and monetize the process.
>
> I have used this exact information to revolutionize my business. I had already written an eBook about Selling on Amazon—but I had

no idea on how to promote it or how to make money from it. This is where Jim Cockrum comes in.

After reading Silent Sales Machine, I collected the emails of *just* the visitors of my website. This is all done with the visitor's permission. They can sign up and unsubscribe at anytime.

Just to give an example. Two days after Christmas, a business partner of mine sent me an email telling me that his book was on sale during the holidays. I immediately sent a short note to my email list about the news. 80 people bought the book, and I made over $800 in commissions in *two* days—*just* by sending a short three-sentence email.

That's just one product. I promote products all the time, and I see the commissions continue to roll in. Imagine what happens when my email list continues to grow . . . the possibilities are endless.

Jim's eBook changed my life. Some books have the power to do that. It's rare, but it does happen. This is one of them.

—Nathan H.

For the rest of this section I'm going to assume that you are interested in using a serious email management tool such as AWeber.com or any of the other email services that I've listed in order to make your efforts as automated and efficient as possible.

Here are the basic tools you'll need to understand in order to automate your email marketing system:

1. An email management service

There are two types of email management systems that you could deploy in your business. There are hosted solutions, and then there are solutions that allow you to store all of your data on your own computers (or servers) and send email from your own servers. I'm a big fan of paying a reputable email service to host all of my addresses and manage my accounts for me. There are several benefits in going this route, including:

> Your solution provider ensures that you remain compliant with all current spam laws.

> You don't have to worry about your IP address becoming blacklisted, or other issues surrounding the management of mass email marketing efforts.

> You automatically stay on the cutting edge of new tools and options without having to upgrade your hardware or software to accommodate the changes.

While some marketers enjoy being able to manage their email addresses themselves from their own computers I prefer to leave the "delivery issues" to the professionals because it alleviates so many potential problems from my business. Also, I can export my entire database from my email service provider anytime I want to (and I do so regularly to make a back up). It's not as if they own my email addresses. To me it feels like keeping my money in a bank rather than keeping it under my own mattress, but I can make a withdrawal at any time and move my money freely.

2. Squeeze pages & opt in forms

A squeeze page is a simple one page website designed with one purpose in mind. The purpose is to gather email leads. The most important part of a squeeze page is the opt in form where prospects can fill in their contact information and then begin immediately receiving the follow-up messages that you have preset in your email management account. If you are going to automate your email marketing efforts you will need to send prospects to quality squeeze pages that contain an email opt in form.

Use this link to watch the short video that shows you how to set up a squeeze page or opt-in form without requiring ANY technical skills:

http://www.youtube.com/watch?v=yzdemYscFhY

So how do I use a *squeeze page*?

When I do radio interviews, write a guest article for a blog, comment on other people's blogs, participate on forums, etc. I always sign off by making mention of my "squeeze page" at SilentJim.com.

When someone asks what I do for a living, or if they ask for a business card, I send them to that site. It's the gateway to a establishing a business relationship with me.

If I were to send first time prospects to a webpage full of random facts and sales pitches trying to sell something, I would have far lower retention and far fewer sales ultimately.

COMPONENTS OF A GOOD SQUEEZE PAGE:

- Easy to spell *and* hard to misspell domain name.

- The entire page fits easily on one screen. No scrolling required.

- Give something of high perceived value away for free in exchange for a lead

- Short bullet point benefits of "opt-in" clearly stated

- Make sure the prospect knows that you'll be sending them regular, relevant information (This can all be set up one time and put on auto-pilot.)

3. Moving prospects from list to list automatically

As prospects become customers, and then customers become "VIP customers" they will begin receiving different types of email messages from you. Ideally you will have established "automation rules" inside of your email management account so that as prospects shift from one list to another, it can occur automatically. For example you can tie your website checkout system to your email management service and automatically move any prospect onto the "recent customer" list when they make a purchase from you.

4. Your follow up messages

As new prospects are added to your email lists you can begin sending them a series of preset messages that arrive sequentially. Sometimes this is referred to as a "drip campaign." Any email management system like the ones I've already told you about can accommodate such a set up.

Some tips for your follow up email message campaigns

Keep it short

A great rule of thumb with email is to always keep it short. Even if you have a great article, newsletter, or other important information to share, you should always keep your email communications short and sweet. For example, when I write a great blog post it's rare that I'll send the entire blog post out in an email broadcast. Instead I'll write a short description of the article in a couple sentences and then include a link for more information in my email broadcast. This type of broadcast message is far less likely to generate spam complaints, and it will also increase the traffic to my blog where I can present the information in a more attractive fashion. On the blog I can interact with the readers in the comment section of my blog post.

HTML is pretty, but I don't do it

There is an ongoing debate about plain text email versus HTML graphic "pretty" messages. I fall firmly in the camp in favor of simple plain text messages as do most other marketers who I work with. Email management services like to try to sell other services (and some of them even throw it in for free), but I still don't use HTML "pretty messages." I won't go into all of the reasons here, but a couple of the strongest arguments I have are the fact that HTML email messages are clearly more likely to get caught in spam filters, and they also instantly identify you as being "a business" and not "a person." I try to keep my email communications personal and friendly. I want my subscriber to completely forget the fact that 100,000 other readers are also reading the same message they are. A text message looks like the email they just got from grandma, and I want it that way. If I want to send something fancier to my customers, I simply include a link to the fancy website, but I don't send them a fancy email. I know this approach isn't right for every business, but it's a perspective to keep in mind and it works very well for me.

I actually surveyed my email list when it was around 8,000 members and I found that 85% of my readers preferred to get a plain text newsletter over an HTML newsletter. To this day, I still send out a plain text newsletter followed up by an email containing a link to the online version the following day. I do the shorter second mailing just in case the longer email got caught in a spam filter.

What do I send my subscribers?

When you first begin using email automation you'll need to established a series of short, powerful, informational messages that can be sent out in a series over time. There should be a gap of a few days in between each message, and your messages should be 70–80% informational, and only 20–30% relevant sales pitch (at most). I'd even suggest that the first several messages do absolutely no selling whatsoever and instead you give away a bunch of great relevant content that builds the customer's trust in your creativity and leadership in the niche market you are writing about.

Dedicate a couple of days to sitting down and thinking through the 20 most useful, and most relevant topics that your prospects are likely interested in, and then put together short email messages that point your prospects to further information on those subjects. The full article could be on your blog, or you could make your point quickly in a short email article. If you aren't sure what to write about, then conduct a survey of your current "top customers" to find out what most interests them. Over time you can always add to the series of messages as well. Once you have this task complete you'll have a virtual "top salesman" in place who will be winning people over little by little with quality information and advice while asking nothing in return. When it comes time to make a sale, your customer will be more than ready to listen to what you have to say (if they don't track you down first because of all the great info you've been sending them!)

Don't get salesy . . .

Referring customers to a popular blog article that you've written (or that someone else has written) and asking them what their thoughts are on the article is a great example of an informational message that leads to interaction and then builds trust. Every new customer gets the same series of email, and they all get sent to the same article, and they all get to see the comments and interaction occurring, etc. This builds a sense of community and trust among your subscribers. It shows them who you are and what you are all about and that they aren't alone. Ask plenty of open ended questions in these messages as well and engage with those that respond. Your email communication shouldn't feel like a company brochure, but instead like a conversation with friends. I want you to blend in with the rest of the messages that your prospects *want* to see in their inbox. For this reason I also suggest that you use your name and not a biz name in the "from" field.

As I've attended various conventions and Internet related events around the world it has been interesting to see how powerful and effective my email automation efforts have been in solidifying my name and reputation in the minds of my readers. It's not uncommon to have people walk up to me and reference an email from me that they got a few days ago, and they'll begin discussing it with me. The fact is though I wrote that email and article over two years ago, inserted into my "follow up sequence," and yet the recent reader thinks that I just recently wrote and sent them that article. This is a powerful phenomenon that nearly any business can and should put use.

Is it all really worth it?

The beauty of automating your email follow-up sequence is that you can do it one time and then leave it all on autopilot indefinitely. Each new prospect who signs up will begin getting a long series of relationship building messages from you and you will reap the rewards if done correctly. If this sounds like too much work, let me remind you of a couple things. If you are going to build a relationship with a prospect, it is going to take multiple contacts with them. This is likely something you've heard before now, right?

Marketing studies have been telling us for years that it takes multiple points of personal contact with prospects before they begin to trust a business or organization. Wouldn't it be better if you could alleviate some of the responsibility of these "multiple contacts" by automating the process somewhat or entirely? Do the work one time and then reap the reward indefinitely. This is the best kind of business strategy.

A winning email strategy

Remember, the most important factor in the success of your email marketing campaign will be your ability to establish trust and rapport with your audience over time. If you fire out a series of sales pitch messages, your email marketing efforts will be a failure. Since the entire process is automated, you can afford to win your customers over slowly by giving them fantastic content and quality tips spread out over multiple messages before you even attempt to sell them anything.

Grow that List!

In my own online businesses, I focus heavily and strategically on constantly growing my email lists with a steady stream of new prospects. Every day I add a minimum of 100 to 200 new prospects into my various email "lead funnels." This level of continuous growth does not happen by accident. I've set up several systems that drive this type of traffic to my email opt in pages.

While every organization and niche market will be a little different, there are several effective strategies that can be used to grow an email list by anyone.

Here are several strategies I personally use along with a brief description of each. You'll find further information about many of these strategies throughout this book.

Partnering in creative ways with those who already have an email list

One of the most powerful strategies for quickly growing your own email list is to find creative ways to partner with those who already have a large email list that contains good potential prospects for your business. These types of cooperative partnerships are often called joint ventures or JV's. If you are starting out without any email list of your own, you will have to be creative in how you approach potential partners. You will have to find a way to make the list owner (a.k.a. the "gatekeeper") look good or earn a nice income from your brief partnership in order for them to be interested in allowing you access to their list.

For example, you might create a high-quality special report and allow the list owner to put their name on the cover as your co-author. Interviewing them and requesting that they share it with their own list is also a great idea. Next, the list owner passes the report or interview out to their entire email list. This makes them look good, and you will grow your email list because of the call to action that is found inside of the special report. The best call to action is something like an offer for more content, or free updates of the special report. Here's a blog post on the topic of connecting with "big hitters" with big lists:

http://www.jimcockrum.com/blog/?p=2113

Writing quality articles

Creating quality content and distributing it far and wide online is useful for more than just generating traffic or recognition for your name and websites. I feel strongly that the best "signature line" that any article can have is a link to a squeeze page or opt in page so that the readers of the article can instantly join your email list if they are interested in the content that they've just read. I would rather have one new email subscriber as a result of someone reading my article as opposed to 100 random website visitors who only stop by my site and are then gone forever.

Submitting quality videos to popular video hosting services

The statistics are astounding. People are increasingly consuming more and more online video content. Rather than have your videos viewed once and then lose the prospect/viewer forever, why not include an invitation to join your email list as a strategic part of every video you produce?

Keeping an active blog

In my opinion the fastest way to measure the effectiveness of a blog is to ask one simple question. How many loyal readers does it have? If a blog has a significant number of readers, yet there is no email capture activity occurring, the blog owner is throwing away literally thousands or possibly even millions of dollars of potential business or publicity. The best call to action for any blog is to encourage blog readers to join the email mailing list. Perhaps the only thing you will ever use those email addresses for is to notify your fans each time there is a new article, but the time will come when you will certainly find it very helpful to have instant access to your entire audience for some other purpose.

Swap blog articles with those who have popular blogs

It's quite common for bloggers to request a blog article swap with other bloggers in the same niche area of interest. You should pursue this type of blog swap activity, but with a twist. Whenever you provide an article to another blogger be sure to include an invitation to join your email newsletter list as part of the article. You'll likely need to ask the permission of the other blogger before doing this, but typically they will agree because most people don't mind and don't care (or even understand) email marketing and how powerful it is.

Creating simple information products for wide distribution online

I'm often asked why I am such a big fan of distributing free content online. The reason is quite simple. If you can pass out quality free information on the Internet, then you can easily convince your prospects to give you an email address. From there it's just a matter of time before you win them over and convince them that you are the "go to" expert on your niche topic of interest. The more free quality content that you can distribute on the Internet, the more likely you are to pull in the types of prospects that your business needs. There is a lot of free information on this topic on my blog at JimCockrum.com, and there's a great course we created as well about writing your own books and info-products as well at ProvenSelfPublishing.com

SEO efforts

While I'm not a big fan of spending a whole lot of energy or money on search engine optimization efforts, I can tell you that the best use of any exposure you do wind up getting is to generate as many email prospects as you possibly can.

I've long predicted the demise of the concept of "SEO" as it gives way to the incoming wave of quality content that is replacing it as the preferred way to rank well and get noticed online. Check out my blog at JimCockrum.com for more on my thoughts on "SEO". I have an entire section dedicated to my simple, yet proven system of Search Engine Optimization.

HERE'S A SAMPLE ARTICLE: http://www.jimcockrum.com/blog/2012/10/22/latest-evidence-of-the-extinction-of-seo-the-seo-pros-are-abandoning-ship/

I also discuss "SEO" in the "where not to start" section in <u>Chapter 5</u> of this book—one of my favorite chapters.

The best use of free press

On those occasions where you or your business are featured in some type of press interview, article or television appearance you need to be prepared. If you are allowed to mention a reference to one of your websites or services, the best thing you can possibly mention is a simple squeeze page designed to gather the email addresses of prospects in exchange for additional information on the topic that you were covering. In my own business, the website <u>SilentJim.com</u> typically serves this purpose. Giving away a high quality information product before you even ask for an email address is also a strategy that is gaining popularity as people become more protective of their contact information.

Ask your email subscribers to forward your messages

As your email list begins to grow there is a synergy effect that will begin to take place. If you are sending out good information there is a good chance that your subscribers will forward the information on to other friends and colleagues who might also benefit or enjoy your mailings. You can multiply the effect by intentionally encouraging them to distribute your information within each email that you send. Make it as easy as possible for new subscribers to join your mailing list as part of each message that you send out. For example, in each of my newsletters I say, "If someone forwarded you this email please take a moment to visit <u>SilentJim.com</u> so that you can get on our free mailing list as well."

Invite every buying customer to join your list

Perhaps the best time to invite someone to join your mailing list is at the point of purchase. Some examples: a sign hung near the register of a retail store, a printed invitation at the bottom of each receipt, or even trained staff who verbally explain your email "customer appreciation" program to each new customer. Any of these tiny procedure shifts can reap huge benefits in growing your email list and eventually having a huge impact on your business.

Get creative with your account names

Whenever possible I use the name "SilentJimDotCom" as my account name or "handle" for services or forums that I join. You never know when a new subscriber will lead to thousands of dollars of new business, so it can really pay to get every extra bit of attention to your squeeze page and email list that you possibly can.

Keeping your content fresh and your audience interested

One of the most effective ways to establish yourself as an expert and grow a loyal following among your subscribers is to publish a regular newsletter, but . . .

It's a fact that few people have time to do a regular newsletter of any kind.

One of the beautiful things about autoresponders is that you can set up messages ahead of time and schedule them to go out automatically at predetermined time intervals for all new subscribers.

This means that you can sit down one day and type out 52 short, relevant, friendly messages and upload them to your AWeber account. You can then set AWeber to send out one message every week to each new subscriber who joins your list.

Congratulations! You are now contacting every lead on your list once per week and building an autopilot relationship with them.

About email newsletters

Assuming you have the time to commit to the process, one of the easiest ways to stay in touch with your prospects and customers is to have a regularly published email newsletter. For the past several years my own newsletter has been one of my strongest sources of income and influence. Hundreds sign up or "opt in" to my various mailing lists at multiple "entry points" including every website I own.

In my case my newsletter is a simple text-only email that is sent to the customers and prospects who have asked to join my mailing list. Over the years I've had hundreds of thousands of people join that list. Not everyone will stay on the list forever, but those who have stuck around for a long time have developed a great relationship with me and my business.

I'll go through some of the excuses and issues I've run into when I've suggested that clients or students of mine begin using email newsletters in their business:

"Aren't newsletters a waste of time usually?"

One of the worst things that could happen with your newsletter project is that it would take on a life of its own and become a project that's done simply because it's always been done. It reminds me of the old corporate newsletters that I used to get when I worked for a "real company." Once every month the newsletter would show up on my desk and I'd watch as everyone nonchalantly dropped their copy of the newsletter into the trash unless it just so happened that their name or department had been featured that week somehow, and then they'd read that one article. The newsletter simply served the purpose of justifying somebody's job position and provided little other value. That is not what your newsletter should become. If it does, then cancel it or change it.

The success of your newsletter can easily be measured by asking two questions:

1. Are your readers happy to get it and then passing it eagerly on to others?

2. Is it generating quality leads and sales for your business with a high ROI for your efforts?

If not, then you are doing something wrong.

The ROI on my newsletter efforts is astronomical. In some cases I've taken 15 or 20 minutes to create an interesting short article teaching a new concept while also selling a related relevant product to my audience. Within a few hours I've made thousands of dollars and the money continues to trickle in over the next several days as the late readers come in.

It's not the newsletter article that was the magic behind those results. It's the trusting relationship with my audience and the size of my audience that are the real factors. The lesson is that you should be building a solid relationship with an ever growing audience. If the newsletter helps you do that, then it's a worthwhile effort that will pay off in big ways for nearly any business.

Don't think of it as a "newsletter"—think of it as a quick, informational point of contact with your customers and prospects.

"I don't know what goes in a good newsletter!"

Your budget, resources, time and business model are all factors in establishing your newsletter. Perhaps the greatest advice I can give you is to ask your customers what they want before you start your newsletter efforts and then keep asking them what they want once you have it established. As simple as this advice might seem to be, I'm pretty sure that most businesses that start a newsletter skip this step entirely. The best source of ongoing content will also be your "reader" base.

You'll know you are onto something when your readers start sharing your content with others. You can know how well your newsletter project is going by monitoring how frequently your newsletter is passed around to other new readers. As part of every newsletter I send out, I invite my readers to forward the newsletter to other people that they think it might help. As a result, each newsletter generates many new email subscribers for me. If this doesn't happen for you, then you need to reevaluate your newsletter efforts.

In order for your newsletter to be worthy of being "passed around" you'll need to think from your customer and prospect's perspective on the topics that you include. Don't waste your time in your newsletter telling your readers how wonderful you are or how great your business is. A newsletter will be evaluated on the quality of the content alone.

When it comes to email, remember—shorter is *better* than longer. Many of my email newsletters can easily fit on one computer screen. There will be 3 or 4 articles at most, and each of them have only a blurb with a link to a website, blog or article for more info on the topic being discussed.

"Does delivery have to be regularly scheduled in order for it to be effective?"

In my opinion the frequency of your communication with your audience via newsletter is of negligible importance. The real factors of your success are the quality of content, and your ability to engage your audience in beneficial conversations. Send your readers to your blog, or even other websites that don't belong to you so that they can get all the best information possible on any given subject. It's this type of honest interaction that will build customer loyalty. Once you have that loyalty established, your customers won't really care how often you publish. Your newsletter will become an extension of your other content creating efforts not unlike your blog, your Facebook page, or your twitter account.

After having maintained my own email lists for nearly a decade now, I have learned several things about what does and doesn't work. If you are considering starting an email newsletter, keep these ideas in mind:

- When writing a newsletter be sure to put in indicators that help your readers to know that the content is current. This is the opposite advice that I gave you concerning any automated "follow-up" messages (also called an email "drip campaign). Your automated follow-up messages will be the same for every subscriber, no matter how far into the future they might join your list. In contrast, your newsletter "blast" is a one time relevant snapshot of current issues and events—so including specific dates, times and time sensitive info is acceptable and beneficial.

- You don't have to be a writer in order to have a very effective email newsletter. Your email newsletter could easily consist of a short message and a link directing your readers to your latest video posted on YouTube. You could also simply record yourself talking about your subject matter and then upload that audio (MP3 or WAV file) to the web, and link to it in your newsletter. I use the term "newsletter" loosely, and I'm not even sure I like the word all that much to describe your broadcasted email communications. Just because I call my weekly mailings a "newsletter" does not mean I deliver a traditional newsletter-looking email to my prospects every week.

- Your newsletter does not have to look fancy in your reader's inbox. I actually discourage my students and clients from using fancy templates when sending email. It's okay to link to a fancy looking newsletter from inside your email newsletter, but the disadvantages of using HTML templates is well-documented, in my opinion.

- The best source of ideas for content in your newsletter is your reader base. Survey them frequently to ensure that you are staying relevant and to get new ideas for content.

- Long email newsletters just don't work. If you have three or four great articles to share with your audience in your email newsletter, please don't send them all in one long email! You should instead include short excerpts from each article along with a link where your readers can go to read the full article (ideally on your blog). This will increase your overall readership and will also make your messages far more likely to make it through the spam filters. Spam filters are used on all major email services and they ALL tend to block "long" emails more frequently than they block "shorter" emails.

- Try not to go more than two—three weeks or so in between contacts with your email list. Setting up automated "follow-up" messages will help ensure that your readers are hearing from you frequently and that they are receiving good content.

- There is no such thing as 100% delivery, 100% open-rates, 100% happy subscribers, or 100% "spam accusation freedom." It's all part of the game. Remember—as long as you are *only* dealing with subscribers that have expressed a specific interest in receiving email from you, you are safe to use email as a promotional tool, but there is nothing "perfect" about email, as we all know. Important messages will sometimes get lost or blocked, people will forget who you are or why they subscribed, lazy subscribers will click the spam button instead of unsubscribing, and you will get occasional complaints from people that think you should be doing things differently. This is all just part of maintaining a one-to-many marketing project such as an email newsletter. I had to learn to have a bit of a thick skin. It's a life skill that all entrepreneurs must develop.

- While your prospects certainly expect you to try to sell them things in your newsletters, keep your ratio of content to sales pitch at about 80/20. This means 80% of what goes into every newsletter is purely informational content. Once you've established the "tone" of your email messaging, stick with it. I had to learn this lesson the hard way. My email communications with my readers is typically about 90% business related and only 10% personal and other topics. In one particular newsletter a few years ago I spent an unusual amount of time discussing an important family/personal issue. While I received an overwhelming amount of supportive response from my readers, I also received a record high level of spam complaints. I could probably interpret this as either being positive or negative, but instead I'm just presenting it to you as the reality of having an established expectation level. Once you go outside of the "norm," you can expect a response that may not be what you were planning on. I now keep a separate list of email addresses that consists of those subscribers who are interested in more personal communication. These "personal" followers all still get my newsletter, but they also get other more intimate details about my life, their opinions on important political issues, etc. It's entirely optional of course, but that type of discussion isn't nearly as welcome on my larger general email list. (For details on joining my "personal" mailing list visit: http://www.jimcockrum.com/blog/?p=1775)

- Learn to stay on topic. I see many email marketers falsely assume that their subscribers are interested in all topics even loosely related to the original content that they signed up for. Proceed with great caution into these types of subjects. Before you blast a questionable article or offer out to your entire list, you should probably test it on a handful of subscribers first and see what their response and reaction is. Just because you've earned the right to be influential in one area of your subscribers' lives does not mean you've earned the right to influence them in all of the other related (or heaven forbid entirely unrelated) areas. Respect the boundaries or your readers will drop out—or worse yet, click the spam button. It's just human nature.

- If you have a new topic you'd like to introduce to your readers, allow them to voluntarily add themselves to the new mailing list. This sort of segmentation makes it far easier to communicate with your list. You can *never* be "over-segmented." It's an established rule of email marketing and I just gave you a great example of this with the previous bullet point.

- You don't have to stick to a predetermined schedule for your newsletter. While I tried to get my newsletter out every week I've never had anyone complain when I skipped a week or two on occasion. People are busy and they aren't going to mind and very few will even notice if they don't get their newsletter.

- If the newsletter isn't making you money, or building customer loyalty that leads to increased sales in some way, then it is a waste of time and your efforts should be reevaluated. Email marketing done correctly is very lucrative as well as being a great experience for the customers.

- As you add new editions of your newsletter be sure to post them online somewhere where they can be seen and indexed by the search engines. The email management service I use (AWeber) does this for me automatically as do most other email delivery tools.

DO THIS: Take my step by step video course about growing massive & loyal email lists by visiting: ListBuildingClass.com

3.2 Embrace Simple Video Now

YouTube has now firmly established itself as far more than just an entertaining video hosting site. It is now a viable search engine for an unimaginable amount of topical video-based content and it's one of the most popular destinations on the Internet. The best part of all is that it's 100% free to use and anyone can upload content. Get yourself established on YouTube now.

If you aren't putting yourself on YouTube, you aren't in the game as much as you should be at this point and you are only falling further behind. No matter what business you are in, if you need more customers than you have now, YouTube is a good place to start making your presence known.

Since my middle son was 10 he's been posting simple video on YouTube.com and within a short time he was able to gather hundreds of thousands of views and thousands of followers on his YouTube account without any help from me. He didn't set out to accomplish these things, he just turned on a video camera and recorded himself doing things like tinkering on his guitar, playing video games, or riding his skateboard. His spelling was atrocious, he didn't try to use the right "keywords," and he has no idea why all of it is getting so big so fast. My point is, if a 10-year-old with a borrowed $100 video camera can create a virtual empire online, why aren't you getting your message out on YouTube?

As with all highly trafficked sites, my advice is typically the same. Be authentic, be creative, and generate leads into your sales funnel by providing valuable content and advice. YouTube is no exception.

In most of the videos that I put on YouTube, I will have a very gentle call to action at some point in the video. This call to action typically invites the viewer to join my email mailing list. Sometimes I give away free downloadable information products as part of the video presentation as well. I don't always have a business purpose in mind when putting content on YouTube, however. One of my most watched videos is one that shows about how to get a high score on a fun online paper airplane game. With the tens of thousands of viewers who I've received to my paper airplane video, I'm sure some of them have noticed my other videos as well.

From a marketing perspective, I find that the most powerful videos are the ones that let you into the "real world" of the person making the video. I'm talking about being authentic. Some of the most popular content on YouTube is the simple stuff. These are the videos that make it easy for the viewer to connect and relate with the maker of the video. Using too many slick graphics, intros, great backgrounds, etc., can actually work against you depending on what your purpose is. This should be encouraging to those who are nervous about creating video content. Spend some time on YouTube checking out popular videos on topics related to your niche interest. You'll quickly see what I mean about the "authentic videos" rising to the top.

How can I go viral with my videos?

By now you've likely heard the term "viral video." When a video begins to get a lot of attention and traction and is being passed around social networks, it is said to have gone "viral."

Of the tens of thousands of videos that are uploaded to YouTube.com daily, what is it about a handful of them that makes them go "viral"?

Several people have attempted to identify a formula, or they have claimed to be able to make it happen repeatedly, but few have achieved any sort of predictable consistency. There are some common elements, though. These elements include videos that:

- Make people laugh

- Are cutting edge with their content or delivery

- Surprise the audience

- Feature an uplifting message

- Are cute (kids, animals)

- Tell a compelling story

- Are short (less than a 2-3 minutes)

- Establish you as *entertaining* or as an *expert*—ideally *both*!

While many of these factors can be fairly hard to achieve intentionally, you should constantly be alert and aware of events and circumstances around you that may lend themselves to being content in a viral video.

A more predictable strategy for gaining attention on YouTube.com is to focus on creating a consistent stream of useful content that includes a clear call to action (e.g. "join our mailing list"). Even if only a handful of people ever see your video in the first year, there could easily come a time in the future where the subject matter of your video becomes fodder for a larger conversation and at that point it could get passed around virally. As long as the content of the video you create has some useful value, or is entertaining, then it is worth having been made.

TESTIMONY: A simple video success story:

One of my newsletter readers, Tracy Hanes, harnessed the power of online video as a marketing tool when he founded his consulting company a couple years ago.

Within a short time he had several major clients approaching him and landed hundreds of thousands of dollars in business training within months.

His only strategy?

Post simple videos on YouTube.com using keywords related to his niche market in the description. These videos quickly showed up on Google for the desirable keywords that he had used in his descriptions.

He produced all the videos himself with no editing except the basic editing features of his inexpensive handheld Flip and Kodak video cameras. The video content is as simple as a guy sitting at his desk talking to an inexpensive video camera.

I asked Tracy what his secrets were in gaining so much attention from the "right people" with his videos and he told me, "I target keywords and do some research. I could literally pick a Google page and place a video there to get first page listing thanks to the power of video."

It's worth noting that none of Tracy's videos have "gone viral," attracting thousands or millions of viewers, but nonetheless they have been highly effective. The several sample videos he sent me had been viewed only a few dozen times each on YouTube.com, but they were working for him very well as they were bringing him the exact kinds of viewers he needed!

The results?

Tracy's business has grown in two years to include three key officers and their business in the most recent year is 1200% larger than their first successful year.

Tracy's "Zero Injury Institute" was established in order to provide "Safety Leadership Concepts" and services to companies in the Industrial Safety niche.

Make video even if you have a face for radio

You don't have to spend very much time on YouTube.com to discover that it's not just the "pretty and articulate people with nice editing skills" who are making videos. If you are going to achieve expert status online, then you'll need to get over whatever fears you have of making and using online video. Remember, it actually works against you to try to be too slick and too polished when presenting your ideas using online video. More than ever before, prospects appreciate online experts who are real and who deliver useful content regardless of how slick the presentation is. This isn't to say that you should ignore quality altogether when producing video, but you should never be discouraged from putting up content that you are worried is less than perfect.

I realize that some people are very shy about appearing on camera. If that's you, I have some good news. It doesn't have to be *your* face or your voice featured in the video content that you create. Your viewers are much more interested in the content of the video than in the details of whose face and whose voice is appearing. Many of my most effective videos contain no "face time" at all, but instead show the viewers screenshots of different websites and online tools that I'm demonstrating. When creating online tutorial types of videos, I use Camtasia (a bit pricey), or SnagIt (almost as good, and far less pricey) software to capture and record both the contents of the website that I'm viewing, as well as my own voiceover commentary.

A great example of the power of online video can be found in the story of Ted Williams. Ted was a homeless man in early 2011 until a caring passerby took the time to record Ted's incredible voice and posted the video to YouTube. Within 2 days, the video had 5 million views and Ted had multiple high profile job offers. By Ted's own admission he has only a "face for radio," but the power of viral video gave him a new lease on life.

TESTIMONY: Another success story thanks to simple video and some basic Internet Marketing skills:

We brought online marketing to the stone age.

We launched a website selling "barefoot" sandals. It's a modern take on a 10,000 year old idea.

Currently we are selling over 400 pairs of Invisible Shoes every month, grossing over $15,000, and still growing. We're about to launch 4 new products (that our customers have been begging for), so we expect those numbers will increase dramatically in the next couple months, even though we'll be selling sandals in the winter.

We've also had 50 retailers sign up to carry our products (and our plan is to get over 500 in our first year with a retail product).

We made our first sale 16 hours after we launched the site.

My wife and I quit our day jobs 3 months later.

Now we're working with a group of consultants who helped build Reebok from < $1,000,000 to an 8-figure business.

A lot of the promotional tactics we learned at OfflineBiz.com have been relevant for our non-local business. Hearing Jim Cockrum extol the value of submitting to video sites was an inspiration to make a lot of videos and we are gearing up to make even more.

The two biggest things we did to promote the site were:

1. Participating on forums where people were already talking about barefoot running. We didn't pitch our product. We just joined in on the conversation and had a simple signature file at the end of each post that let people know we had free DIY videos on our website.

2. Sharing how-to videos on YouTube and other video sites . . . where I showed how to make our product without ever buying our product! I gave complete plans to do it yourself with items you might have around the house.

The lessons:

One of the things that I've found is: people respond to people. That is, the more you (and your employees) can be visible, accessible, and available online, the more your potential customers can relate to you. And the more they relate to you (or, again, the people in your company), the more connected to you and your products they feel. And the more connected they feel, the more they want to do business with you. You can't make this a *strategy* . . . you simply have to do it honestly.

Don't be afraid to give away a lot of free information—I've had dozens of runners come up to me at races and show me the shoes they've made following my instructions. While they didn't buy anything from me, they've referred others who have. And, maybe, some day, I'll offer something they can't make on their own and they'll become customers (actually, it's guaranteed that I'll have that product to offer them).

—Steven Sashen
  Invisible Shoe

There is so much good free content online regarding making videos to get your message out. One of the best places to pick up the skills you need is by watching "how to do video" videos right on YouTube. We've learned so many skills quickly by seeking out true professionals on the YouTube.com platform.

> **A CHALLENGE FOR YOU:** Do whatever it takes to get a video posted on YouTube.com. No excuses, no delays. This chapter has given you all the confidence, tools, and advice you need—go make it happen now if you've never done it before.

3.3 Let Someone Else Do the Hard Stuff

If you find yourself working in your business more than you are working *on* your business, then something is out of order and you won't grow as quickly or as large as you should be.

One of the vital skills you'll need to acquire if you are going to live out the "Silent Sales Machine" lifestyle is *outsourcing*.

While it's true that no one can complete a task *exactly* the way you would, it's also true that struggling to maintain control of every aspect of your business will keep you small and slow moving.

For example, one of my rules I teach eBay sellers is "Never Touch Box Tape". What does this mean? It means that you can pay a neighbor kid a few dollars per hour and free up a *bunch* of your time if you let someone else pack and ship your boxes. Don't ever allow yourself to get caught up in the mundane tasks.

Any repetitive or technically challenging projects that you find yourself trying to tackle on your own should be passed off to someone else who can do the job more easily, faster and in most cases better than you could ever do it yourself. Your time is the premium asset that you should be protecting when it comes to making business decisions. The more time you can free up, and the less money you can spend freeing it up, the more successful you'll become and the faster your business will grow.

Outsourcing (using sites like oDesk.com, vWorker.com and Elance.com) is becoming a vital component of many successful businesses on and offline. Regardless of where you stand on the idea of using help from other countries outside of your own, the fact is that there are many skilled programmers, writers, web designers, and hosts of other talented people all over the planet. When I have a task to complete for my business, I don't limit my talent pool to only those who live inside of my own country. I open the job up to all eligible candidates.

Few business owners realize it, but you can hire *amazingly* hard working, talented, honest, reliable help for a few dollars per hour in the Philippines. Filipinos love the U.S. dollar (and the Euro) because the currency goes *so far* in their country.

A family of four which has a head of household making just a few dollars per hour can live quite comfortably by local standards, and steady jobs are very hard to find there currently.

In the Philippines there is an overabundance of talented, English speaking, skilled tech savvy workers ready and willing to go to work *today* making your Internet business grow even while you sleep. I've hired web designers, writers, email customer service agents, and content distribution experts from the Philippines.

The Filipino culture is characterized by being hard working, honest, and they don't resent their foreign employers as some people might suspect they would. They are grateful for the work in most cases. Typically they love the chance to do meaningful work and they will thank you frequently for the chance to prove they are worthy of your trust.

> **DO THIS:** John Jonas is my "go to" expert on all things related to hiring help from other countries. He's given me several pointers over the years and we recorded a good audio on the subject covering everything you need to know about hiring someone from the Philippines. Visit this link to get access to the training webinar we conducted:
>
> http://www.jimcockrum.com/blog/?p=693

I see many business owners become bogged down in doing the day-to-day tasks that could and should be passed off to someone else's capable hands. Think through the tasks that you perform yourself on a day-to-day basis. Are any of those tasks ones that could be passed to someone else if they were willing to work remotely for a few dollars per hour? If so, you should be focused on transitioning those responsibilities to someone else.

In my own business I am constantly evaluating the way I spend my time, and I've given away several of the mundane tasks that can easily clutter my day. I have a handful of part-time helpers locally who helped me run my business as well as workers in other nations doing Internet-based work for me. I think of all of it as "outsourcing." Once I established the value of a business hour of my time, it was easy to justify investing some money freeing up my time.

What work should you as "the owner" be doing? Focus on working *on* your business instead of *in* your business. Think, create, plan and do only the stuff you love to do. Try to leave the rest to others. Even if you love the work you are doing, be sure that you are dedicating significant time to "replacing yourself." If you are unable to remove yourself from the equation of the day to day responsibilities of your business, you will never be able to take a break without losing income and you'll lose the ability to focus on expanding your business to the next level. There is also the factor of making your business transportable so that a new owner could buy and take over the business if it ever became necessary or desirable.

If you are trapped in the mentality of thinking that you are the best person to tackle every aspect of your business, then your business will never be very large, and it will own you as it grows. Do not allow your business to own you. Outsource the tasks that could and should be getting done by someone else.

Interestingly enough, the *only* skill I think you need in order to succeed as a consultant assisting "real world" businesses with their Internet marketing and social marketing efforts is *outsourcing*. At OfflineBiz.com (I'll talk more about that site in a later chapter) we have over 10,000 members who are all building businesses by consulting (assisting) "real world" clients with their marketing. We teach outsourcing skills as being vital to growing your business as profitably as possible. If you try to be the one who does all the "techie" work you will never grow a viable business.

TIP: People with *skills* work for people with *ideas*. Be an idea person.

There's a reason that I only teach my students to learn a handful of basic skills.

You *don't* need to be able to do these tasks:

- build websites

- add content to existing websites

- program

- create graphics

- edit your writing (grammar etc.)

- edit video

- edit audio

- answer customer support email or phone calls

- etc.

All of these tasks and many more can be handled for a few dollars per hour by someone else once you know how to find good help.

As your business grows, outsourcing will become one of only a handful of *vital* skills you'll need to get comfortable with.

3.4 Find Your Audience First

This "Find Your Audience" skill won't seem like a skill at all until I explain myself better, but trust me, this is a *vital* skill if you are to succeed online.

I've seen few success stories among those who lacked this "FYA" skill as I'll call it.

Your entrepreneurial instincts *will not like* this FYA skill, so it may take you some time to develop it (and it will take some work for me to convince you I'm right). Hopefully it's something that will come to you quickly, because it will save you a *ton* of time, heartache and money to learn this lesson early on. If you are to succeed with multiple income streams, you will do well to gain this vital skill.

Let's start with some bad news.

I'll give you a few examples of what I've seen happen over and over to those who lack this FYA skill:

- You'll operate under the false assumption that building a website, creating a product, or writing a book is the *first step* to success online and you'll believe the "experts" and teachers who are trying to sell you system after system to help you do such crazy things. (It's not crazy to do these things . . . but it is crazy to *start* out with any of those activities as your starting point.)

- You are far more likely to develop "shiny object" syndrome where you fall for every guru launch and "step by step" system that promises to teach you to make money online while they are in nearly *all cases* leaving out a *vital* piece of the strategy that virtually ensures your failure before you even begin.

- You'll jump from idea to idea without success all the while blaming yourself for failing. You might even wind up hating the Internet and abandoning the greatest business tool ever invented by mankind!

Sound familiar? I've got more examples of what it sounds like when I hear from those who lack the "FYA" skill.

I get emails all the time from excited newsletter readers or fans of my "stuff" that start out something like this:

> "I've got a great idea and I'm wondering if you think it will work. I want to build a website that does _____ (fill in the blank), or I want to write a book about _____ (fill in the blank) or I want to create a product that helps people who need _____ (fill in the blank). Jim, I'm wondering if you think it's a good idea or not—can you help me market this?"

My opinion on the matter, while probably a bit more accurate than someone with less experience is still just that . . . an opinion.

The real questions are these:

> *How will you FYA (Find Your Audience) online and get them interested and engaged enough to make your idea work?*
>
> *Can this be done without any costly investments or risks?*

These are the types of questions I always fire back at eager online dreamers.

In other words . . .

"Where is your audience?"

When I ask that last question *I'm **not** asking you to identify your target demographic.* For example, your target customer might be single moms with older kids, or married couples with dual careers, etc., but that's *not* the answer I'm looking for. Instead I'm asking you to find out exactly *where* online (what websites) are the kind of people you want to reach already gathering? What websites are they hanging out on? What discussion forums do they use? Who owns a mailing list full of eager engaged fans in your niche? I want to see you come up with a list of *leaders with large followings* (I call these people gatekeepers) and popular *websites* that are used by your target audience.

Reread this entire FYA chapter over and over until it sinks in. Failure to grasp the concept I'm showing means you are looking at 1:1,000 odds of success as opposed to virtually *assured* success.

Once this chapter makes sense to you, read on . . .

The next question is this:

"How will you get the attention of your audience?"

Here's a great blog post that will really drill home these points:

http://www.jimcockrum.com/blog/?p=308

To get the attention of your audience you might have to partner with the "gatekeeper" of that audience in a creative way.

If you are going to do any sort of "niche" marketing on line, here's the fail proof system I've used to succeed on *all* of the projects I've gotten into in the last eight years:

NICHE MARKETING 100% SUCCESS FORMULA:

1. Identify a hot niche market

2. Give that audience great free content to grow your email list (by partnering with a gatekeeper)

3. Ask the audience what else they want

4. *Create a product or website* that meets the needs of your audience

5. Sell outstanding affiliate offers to your audience (no garbage allowed)

6. Automate your list building and prospect follow up efforts

The strange thing about this model is that the "product" isn't first or even second on the list. You aren't building websites, writing books, or creating a product until step four at the soonest (if you ever do it at all—you may just sell affiliate products!)

At the start of <u>Chapter 3</u>, I told you about the best three paths to success online based on my decade of success. I call it my "C.E.S." model—you can use one or all three.

1. C = Consult. Help other business owners apply basic Internet Marketing skills to their business and prosper from your efforts in helping them succeed.

2. E = Expand. Find a profitable niche market, be a leader in that niche and give your followers fantastic content while also selling them products, services, training, or information that is of interest to them.

3. S = Sell Stuff. Sell profitable physical goods through your own site, Amazon or eBay and find creative ways to automate the entire system and grow a huge customer following for future sales.

The FYA principle applies to all three (as do the other skills I've shown you in this chapter).

When selling physical goods for example it makes sense to *go to where the audience is*. This is why I advise most newbies to start on eBay or better yet, Amazon. Don't start out building a website to sell your widgets! Instead go to where the widget shoppers are already hanging out. Your customers are on Amazon and eBay—and if you can't get their attention there, you'll have an exponentially harder time selling products from your own website.

Ignore the advice of section 3.4 at your own peril! If you ignore this piece of advice, your odds of success are about the same as a young actor spending his last $100 for a bus ticket to Hollywood . . . or a young musician strapping his guitar on his back and hitchhiking to Nashville. Sure, many success stories start that way, but millions of very sad stories start that way as well.

In other words . . . *it ain't looking pretty for you if you ignore me on the FYA principle* no matter how "cool" your idea, or how talented you are. Sure, you *might* still make it, but the odds are very stacked against you.

3.5 Work With Great Partners

One of the advantages of living in the time we do as entrepreneurs is the fact that our prospects are gathering in easy to access groups or "communities" at an ever increasing rate.

It's as if each of us as entrepreneurs are a fisherman in a land where new streams and lakes full of fish just keep appearing out of thin air.

The only barrier to accessing these new sources of prospects is our ability to creatively partner with those who own and manage the streams and lakes that we would like to access.

For many businesses niche markets, the customer base is already hanging out online on blogs, websites, and discussion forums related to its target niche market.

A quick search on the major search engines for each of the best keywords associated with your niche will produce several pages of potential partners. Each of these sites are potential partners for you to work with. These websites are the places where your future customers are already hanging out.

You'll find several other websites to add to your targeted list of "potential partners" if you add the word "blog" or the word "forum" to each of your Google, Bing or Yahoo search queries.

Once you have your list, it's time to start forming relationships with each of the targeted sites. Even if you only wind up working with one or two of the fifty sites you find, it will have been well worth the effort.

In some cases, your only option to gain exposure on these target sites will be to purchase advertising, but in almost all cases there are other creative possibilities available to you. Begin an intentional campaign of attracting the attention of the key decision makers on these sites by contributing to their success and by expressing your desire to partner up. Here are some creative ideas to try:

- Try to identify the people behind the website. You need to know who the key players are so that you can form real relationships with them.

- Make useful comments on blog posts or articles on their site or where you find things written about their site elsewhere online.

- Send them links to useful content that may be of interest to them (Google Alerts are great for tracking this, or to track bigger news trends around any given niche or topic use NewsTimeline.GoogleLabs.com).

- Follow the website and more importantly the individual key players who run the site. Follow them on Twitter, Facebook or YouTube and make supportive and relevant comments on the content they post there.

- Get their physical mailing address and send a creative card or gift expressing your appreciation and admiration for what they've done. Don't have an agenda when you reach out—just form a real relationship and give honest feedback.

- Send them great original articles that they can use as content. You don't have to ask permission first—just send it over!

- Find places online where the key players or the website itself is mentioned or discussed. Pay special attention to anyone that says something negative, and make a thoughtful reply defending the key players or the site. Trust me—they'll notice this. For example, a VP of PayPal called to thank me a couple of years ago after I spent some time defending PayPal on an open discussion forum. I had no agenda when writing my comments, but the VP went to great lengths to track me down so he could bounce some ideas off of me and then he sent me a T-shirt. It's good to have friends like that online.

Those types of strategies will help you to win over the key players and influencers at any website—even those "big cold" sites that seem impossible to crack into. You'll slowly earn the right to partner with them in creative ways that others don't have access to.

Finding creative ways to create three-way wins is your next step.

The three-way win

If I had to identify the one concept that has played the greatest role in my success online it would be the idea of a "three-way win". You've heard of "win/win" arrangements before, but I add in a third "winner" to my strategy when it comes to building a quality email list fast, or getting my message of any kind in front of an entirely new audience. By adding in this third "winner," I can then actively seek out win/win/win opportunities. By doing this I have built a virtual online empire.

What is win/win/win?

The win/win/win strategy is easily grasped once you are made aware of the virtually infinite number of new communities and influential leaders which are already established online. By partnering with these online leaders, you can do big things fast. Many businesses are even starting to hire "affiliate managers" just to manage their relationships with powerful online influencers because they recognize that these influential leaders hold the keys to rapid exposure online.

The three parties that must win are:

A. The community (otherwise known as the readers, the subscribers, the members, etc.)

B. The community leader (the guy with influence, the blog owner, the list owner, the guy with the popular website). For this example, let's assume it's a guy with a large targeted email list.

C. *You* (the guy with great information to share that wants more visitors, traffic and eyeballs on his stuff).

The rules of the win/win/win game:

- As long as the community (A) is getting timely, relevant information from their trusted leader (B) they will remain loyal to that source and they will tell others about it in a viral fashion.

- Very few community leaders (B) are so convinced of their own importance as to think that *only* their ideas are good enough to share with their community (A). This opens the door for other "experts" and "content contributors" (*you* [C]) to get in front of the community with the blessing of the leader (B). Most forward looking community leaders (B) actively *seek out* top notch contributors (*you* [C]) to help keep their community happy, and their own reputation intact.

- A good win/win/win makes the community leader (B) look great and helps him grow his audience. It also makes the community (A) very happy and gives them something they want, and gains *you* (C) the exposure you are seeking. If you can accomplish this sequence successfully even a handful of times, you'll have tremendous success online.

- A good community leader (B) always acts as a filter to keep bad content out (the invisible 90% of the job) and let the best content in so that the experience of his loyal community members (A) is protected and strengthened. I've heard this role described as being a "curator of content."

- As a content contributor (*you* [C]) you should *only* work with trusted community managers (B) who have the best interest of their community (A) in mind. Don't do a partnership with anyone who treats their community abusively because your reputation will be tarnished as they eventually go down in flames for abusing their influential position. I've seen it happen many times.

- The best content contributors come from a place of experience, success, motivation, originality and credibility. To the degree that you lack any of those characteristics it will be harder for you to succeed. If you have all or even some of those character qualities you'll quickly move from a contributor to a trusted and respected leader (B). Once you are an influential leader to some degree on your own, you will then find it easier to initiate win/win/win arrangements.

- The better the community leader (B) is at managing his community (A) and the larger the community is, the harder it is for you (C) to get your foot in as a contributor, but it's always worth it in the end. I've had potential partners pursue me for months attempting to get some exposure to my 100,000+ email followers. Most of the time, I turn these people away.

You can see the win/win/win strategy played out just by following my free newsletter or blog. While I do write most of the content, I will occasionally offer up content from guest writers who have contacted me, or those with a fantastic relevant product to offer. The guest writers or product owners get exposure and sales, I get commissions and kudos from readers, and the readers get the content they want. As long as I make sure that I filter the content diligently, the win/win/win continues.

A great recent example is the website ProvenSelfPublishing.com. My parter on that project was Jason Miles. He did nearly all of the content while I did about 15% of it. We share in the sales that are made, and he gets the additional benefit of exposure to my audience. As he promotes the site to his ever growing audience I get additional exposure to new readers as well.

More about joint ventures

My first simple eBook I wrote earned me $600 and about 150 subscribers to my email list on the *first day* I launched it. This was well *before* I had any audience of my own. I simply found an email list owner who had an audience made up of people who I thought might be interested in my book. I offered a 50% cut (an affiliate commission) on all sales made and asked the list owner to send an informational promotion of my book to her email list. This resulted in several sales and also helped launch my online eBook career. I did the same thing multiple more times with other influential leaders in my niche until I had a well established following of my own.

The foundation of much of my early success online came as a result of doing joint ventures with other marketers and websites that were servicing my same customer demographic.

These partners agreed to promote my products, articles and services to their customer base if I would do the same thing for them in return. Over time I've become much more discretionary about who I will enter into such arrangements with. Just because someone is willing to promote my product does not mean I'll be willing to promote theirs. This is because I've learned to protect my audience from any products or information that doesn't resonate with my core principles and message.

If I can find other experts who have a good reputation and high-quality products, I'm very willing to enter into a joint venture partnership with them. If it isn't obvious already, the best way to position yourself for success with joint ventures is to have a large loyal audience. A common phrase in Internet marketing circles is, "He who has the list, wins."

In my opinion one of the greatest indicators of marketing prowess is a large loyal email list of followers who are eager to hear from the owner of that list. There is no stronger position to be in. Find creative ways to partner with these "leaders" and prosper from it!

CAUTION: Pick partners with integrity

1+1=3: Synergy

Some of the best advice that I got early on in my business career was to be very careful about who I partner with. That advice is still very true, but in the Internet age we live in, there are multiple kinds of partnerships that didn't exist before. These new kinds of partnerships present a whole new level of risk and opportunity.

Ten years ago, entering into a business partnership implied a much stronger and legally binding arrangement that was full of risks and involved a great deal of planning, lawyers, paperwork, financial considerations, etc.

When I talk about partnerships in this chapter however, I'm referring to a much less structured type of arrangement. For example, I previously talked about joint venture partners, and "three-way win" partners.

Some of these partnerships are entered into with only a few minutes of research and negotiation involved, and the partnership activity lasts only a few days. In other cases, longer-term partnerships are formed. But in nearly all cases, there is a casual and speedy process of compatibility evaluation and agreement on the terms. Nothing is signed, reputations are the handshake, and business goes forward rapidly.

Those who abuse this simple "unwritten" system go down in flames so quickly that there is a built-in incentive to carefully guard your reputation. Even these "simple" partnerships can lead to trouble though, if your name gets tied to someone who doesn't put their character and customers first.

A PARTNERSHIP SUCCESS STORY: *Would you partner with someone you hardly know?*

I have a partner who shares a 50/50 arrangement on the 12,000+ member strong membership site OfflineBiz.com. Andrew Cavanagh is my partner, yet I have never actually met or spoken to him because we live on opposite sides of the planet. We manage hundreds of thousands of dollars in membership fees and other income annually from our partnership efforts, yet the entire arrangement for our partnership happened in a series of short emails exchanged over the course of a couple days a few years ago.

How is such an arrangement possible?

When I approached Andrew initially, he and I both quickly researched the online reputation and accomplishments of the other party, and it was quickly obvious that the combined skill sets and assets that we brought to the table would produce a great deal of synergy and success. In other words, we knew we'd be successful before we even started. It was just a matter of putting the pieces into place.

Those of us that recognize the power of a strong online reputation now have an advantage over everyone else. A bad reputation stands out online easily. Having no reputation stands out almost as glaringly. Having a great reputation however, is impossible to fake. By establishing your own great reputation and then seeking out simple, complimentary partnerships with others that also have built up a strong online presence and reputation, you can find amazing partners very quickly. Starting your search can be as simple as spending a few minutes searching online using your industry keywords and Google.

If you enjoy these types of topics you'll love my "real book" top seller 101FreeMarketing.com book. It has several other similar ideas regarding creative partnerships.

Concluding Thoughts for Chapter 3

I've just given you some essential skills that will be of great benefit to you no matter what direction you go online. Studying and perfecting these skills (and virtually *no other skills*) will mean you are equipped for unlimited opportunities online.

Let me re-emphasize the point that you can easily get sucked into a "skill cycle" on the Internet and never escape! *You could waste time for years learning how to:*

- build HTML websites

- use Wordpress

- build a blog

- shop for profitable inventory online or retail

- find profitable products to sell

- do "social marketing" all yourself

- edit pictures

- return every customer phone call

- design graphics

- program PHP

- customer support issues

- build membership websites

- update old content

- answer all email yourself

- edit your writing

- ship products faster and cheaper doing it yourself

- drive around town as efficiently as possible buying stuff for your biz

- post content to various sites for maximum exposure

- edit video/audio

- transcribe your video/audio

- etc., etc.

All of these are *time wasters* in my opinion! They are all a vital part of my various businesses, but I don't do *any* of these activities myself, *nor* do I pay a lot of money to have these things done! I partner with great people and have them do the work while we share in the benefits of the results.

Show me someone with a skill (*any* skill) and in ten minutes I'll find someone who is *faster, cheaper, better* (better looking and funner to work with too) . . . all in about ten minutes. If you pursue skills beyond the ones I've listed in this chapter, please do so with extreme caution!

"People with *skills* work for people with *ideas*." —Jim Cockrum

CHAPTER 4

Some "Silent Sales Machine" Business Ideas

Now that I've shown you some of the basic tools that have helped me (and thousands of others) establish solid income streams, let's talk about some specific income models.

The graph on the next page was something I drew on a napkin not too long ago to help illustrate where I thought the real business opportunities are online. Thanks to my friend Thea Woods for turning my scribbles into a nice diagram for all of us and for updating an older version to the above "new improved" version just for this book.

Each dot on the graph represents a business opportunity that is worth familiarizing yourself with. If the biz-op you are considering isn't on this map, there's almost certainly a reason for it!

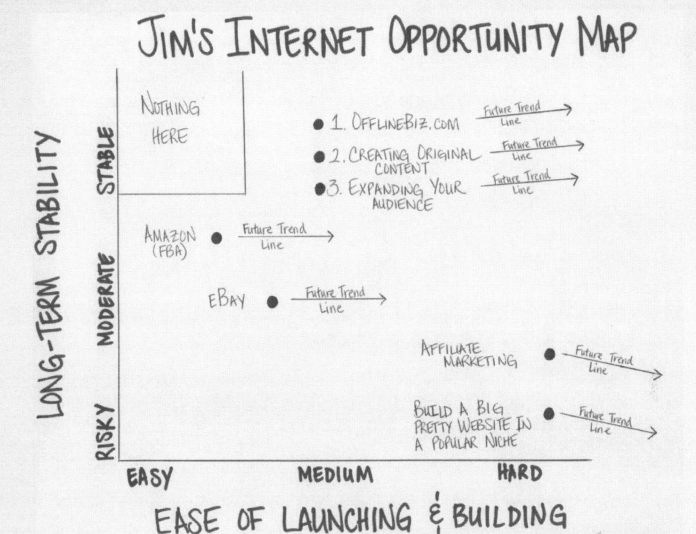

Jim's Internet Opportunity Map

LONG-TERM STABILITY (vertical axis)

- STABLE
- MODERATE
- RISKY

EASE OF LAUNCHING & BUILDING (horizontal axis)

- EASY
- MEDIUM
- HARD

NOTHING HERE

- 1. OfflineBiz.com — Future Trend Line →
- 2. Creating Original Content — Future Trend Line →
- 3. Expanding Your Audience — Future Trend Line →

AMAZON (FBA) ● Future Trend Line →

EBAY ● Future Trend Line →

AFFILIATE MARKETING ● Future Trend Line →

BUILD A BIG PRETTY WEBSITE IN A POPULAR NICHE ● Future Trend Line →

To join the discussion about this "map" and see a bigger picture of it please visit:
http://www.jimcockrum.com/blog/?p=1426

These observations come from over 10 years of experience establishing, consulting with and watching successful online businesses. I stand by the placement of these "dots" after careful consideration of where each opportunity should fall on the map. There is however an interesting debate on my blog about all of this among my readers.

As a reminder—all of the above topics fall into one of the three categories I've mentioned previously:

1. C = Consult. Help other business owners apply basic Internet Marketing skills to their business and prosper from your efforts in helping them succeed.

2. E = Expand. Find a profitable niche market, be a leader in that niche and give your followers fantastic content while also selling them products, services, training, or information that is of interest to them.

3. S = Sell Stuff. Sell profitable physical goods through your own site, Amazon or eBay and find creative ways to automate the entire system and grow a huge customer following for future sales.

To discuss any of these business models with my coaching team please call us at 1.800.994.1792, or jump over to my blog and talk it over with other readers and me:

http://www.jimcockrum.com/blog/?p=1426

TESTIMONY: I just completed six sessions of coaching with one of Jim's coaches who has helped me jump start my new business venture. The coach's in-depth knowledge of the business was instrumental in helping me go from zero to over several thousand in monthly sales within just three months. His ability to listen to my needs and his friendly, clear, and affable communication style made the coaching experience fun as well as educational. I highly recommend coaching to anyone who is serious about learning the online business.

—Dr. C Wolf

To read many other success stories, please visit JimCockrum.com *and click on "testimonials."*

4.1 Content is Cash

I've sold literally millions of dollars of information online. I've sold my own information as well as information put together by others (I get an affiliate commission in those cases). It's all "virtual content." To me, virtual content includes video, articles, eBooks, audios, kindle books, etc.

These items can be given away, sold, or hidden behind membership sites so that only paid customers can gain access.

The beauty of "virtual content" online is that it has *very* high utility for paying customers when created and delivered correctly—but it costs the content creator virtually nothing to deliver. You create it once, and it lives on and on.

For example, I have written books and courses that took a lot of work to complete, but once I was done, the process of selling, delivering and supporting those customers took very little work or effort on my part. It was all automated.

If you aren't in the business of creating content that consumers want and need, then I'm about to talk you into this business model. As long as you pick a niche where there are passionate prospects, it's hard to go wrong.

If you are going to attract loyal followers and prospects online, it all starts with creating good content for them to consume.

What is a "passionate prospect"?

I tell people all the time to pursue their dream and do what they love, but if they want to increase their odds of success 1,000x they need to seek out a niche with "passionate prospects." You'll know you have passionate prospects when you get into a niche market where people can't sleep at night or they wake up each day thinking about your niche. The emotionally charged, polarizing, passionate niche markets are well documented in many cases, but there are many of them. You see the "how to make money," "relationships" and "beauty/fitness" niche markets everywhere for a reason. These are some of the most common and emotionally-charged niche markets.

There are of course thousands of other niche markets to get into. I've coached successful businesses in countless niche markets including real estate, paint ball accessories, guitar pedals, hand-made wreaths, alternate running shoes, and various pet niche markets, just to name a few.

In all cases, your success starts out with choosing a niche where there are enough qualified prospects already eager for more, and already assembling together in groups (at least loosely) somewhere online.

Content is whatever information your prospects want

It's getting harder and harder to force your message into the lives of busy people who are already focused on other things that they care more about. It has become increasingly simple for all of us to surround ourselves with only the content and messages that we wish to receive. We are all annoyed by anything that forces its way into our attention.

This means that great content is not a slick online brochure or fancy video touting all of the features of your latest and greatest products. Instead, great content is simply defined by your prospects as, "exactly the right information I want or need at exactly the right time I need or want it." Ideally, it's also free to consume (until you've proven the value of your content and your prospects are *begging* for more and willing to pay a fair price to get it).

If you can find a way to position yourself as an expert who frequently delivers great content (you'll likely start with "free" content), you won't be able to contain the number of leads and prospects who will beat a path to your door. Your best customers will also become your best salespeople as they spread the word about how great you are.

I've already listed several types of content at the start of this chapter, but let me stress that the *format* of your content (audio, video, eBook, kindle, blog article, etc.) is not nearly as important as the *quality* of your ideas. If you are engaging, helpful, and "shareable" (meaning people want to spread the word once they hear or see your content) then you are all set and the format becomes irrelevant. All forms of content delivery are open to those that have a message that is desirable.

With that being said, let's focus on one of my favorite forms of content.

Books are one of my favorite kinds of content

I believe everyone has a good book or two or fifty in them. Very few people ever get it done, though. That's probably part of the reason why the title of "author" is held in such high esteem.

If the idea of having a "real book" is a bit intimidating, or if you don't feel quite ready for it, consider the option of writing an eBook. When I say eBook, I mean any type of electronic or digitally delivered book. It could be a kindle book, a PDF file, or some other future popular format for the written word that's not yet common.

The eBooks that I've written are simple PDF files that can be sent as an email attachment, or downloaded and easily distributed instantly anywhere in the world where there is an Internet connection. This book you are now reading was likely distributed to you as an eBook. I've sold or given away over 500,000 eBooks, so I'm well versed on the subject.

Writing your first eBook could be as simple as creating a 20 page document and then saving it as a PDF file. A PDF formatted file is preferred because it can be opened by anyone on any computer (Mac or PC). My favorite way to create a PDF is by using the free OpenOffice. org writer software. It's as easy to use as any other word processor, but when you are done creating your document, you just click the PDF button and you are done. If you later have edits or additions for the book, you edit the original file, click the PDF button again, and you have a completely updated PDF file.

My experience with eBooks has been life-changing. I wrote my first 20 page eBook over a decade ago and within just a few weeks my life began to change forever. Having eBooks floating around the Internet has made me a lot of money.

For over 10 years now I've had the privilege of waking up each day, logging on to my computer, and checking the statistics of how many books I sold while I was sleeping. It's a feeling that never gets old. These books are delivered electronically as downloadable files to customers who purchase them from my various websites.

One of the best ways to establish yourself as a credible "thought leader" in any niche market is to create an eBook product. Even if you simply record an interview with other experts in the niche, you will still be perceived as an expert for having completed a book project and the marketing potential is limitless.

An eBook should be a lead generating tool that gives away great content, while establishing your expertise. Don't make it a big sales pitch, and don't fill it with "fluff" content. The customers who buy or even download something for free are expecting a great first impression, so put great information inside. When I sell information it's the starting line for a life long relationship (hopefully) with a new customer. It's not the finish line where I finally made some money. The customer needs to feel like they got 10x the value from the purchase or I've failed them.

SUCCESS STORY: I had ten years experience running a martial arts school. I had started the school from scratch with no credit, no education, and no money—and then I grew it successfully to roughly 200 students. I felt I had a lot to say about the martial arts industry that just wasn't being said in the mainstream publications.

So I wrote a book.

I wasn't willing to settle for getting a few dollars off of each book sale, so I aimed higher.

That's when I started seriously studying how to market products and information online. I encountered a pretty steep learning curve at first, but within a few short years I had overcome any initial challenges and my book had garnered a die-hard underground cult following. I managed this with little if any mainstream press coverage, and well before social media had become a factor in viral marketing. Mostly, I relied on organic search engine traffic and word-of-mouth as well as some PPC.

It's encouraging to know that countless martial arts instructors who followed my book to success are now running successful schools. Without a doubt, that's the most rewarding thing about marketing my ideas as an expert.

And honestly, without folks like Jim Cockrum freely sharing their knowledge and experience about Internet marketing online, I'd never have been able to learn the ins and outs of online marketing. Thanks Jim, and thanks to all the other Internet marketing coaches who helped me along the way who are too numerous to mention here.

—Mike Massie
  small-dojo-big-profits.com

Some thoughts from an eBook veteran

1. You can't have a "protect my ideas" mindset with eBooks because it will work against you.

There is a mentality you'll have to adapt if you're going to be successful as an eBook author. The reality is, your product will be passed around to people who haven't paid for it (if it's any good at all). Just plan on that happening and use it to your advantage. Whenever I create content that I know will be going into an eBook (or anywhere online for that matter), I intentionally include multiple links, references, and stories that all lead the reader back to my websites, blog, mailing lists, etc. By doing this I'm actually ensuring that even the most blatant of copyright violations against my material will actually be a huge marketing boost for my overall business. This is one of the most common concerns that I hear when working with new eBook authors, but once you have the correct mindset you'll quickly realize that it's a non-issue. I actually enjoy seeing my eBook products being "secretly" distributed on piracy download websites. It's all free marketing, from my vantage point. If you want to try and track where your content might be showing up online I suggest you use free Google Alerts (Alerts.Google.com) to track your content. By setting up an alert for key phrases from your work, you can instantly see if someone posts your content to a website.

2. There are many ways to distribute your work. Use them all!

Over 10 years ago I set up a simple website to sell the book you are now reading. The book has been updated 8 times and the website has been updated as well, but the simple website where it all started is still the primary place where my book sells every day. You'll find my books as well on Amazon in various formats, and on Audible.com in audio format. The format and location doesn't matter really—why not use *all* available options when it is so easy to do? If you have to pick just *one* place to start though, start with Amazon. More on that topic at the end of this chapter.

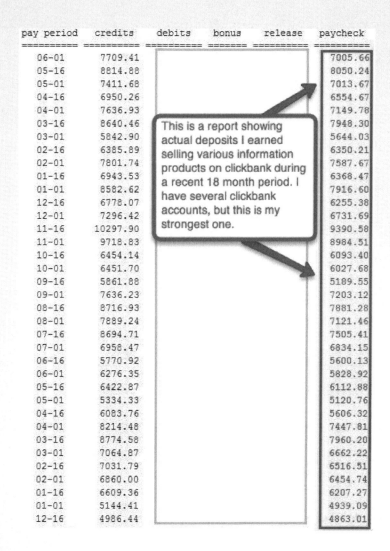

pay period	credits	debits	bonus	release	paycheck
06-01	7709.41				7005.66
05-16	8814.88				8050.24
05-01	7411.68				7013.67
04-16	6950.26				6554.67
04-01	7636.93				7149.78
03-16	8640.46				7948.30
03-01	5842.90				5644.03
02-16	6385.89				6350.21
02-01	7801.74				7587.67
01-16	6943.53				6368.47
01-01	8582.62				7916.60
12-16	6778.07				6255.38
12-01	7296.42				6731.69
11-16	10297.90				9390.58
11-01	9718.83				8984.51
10-16	6454.14				6093.40
10-01	6451.70				6027.68
09-16	5861.88				5189.55
09-01	7636.23				7203.12
08-16	8716.93				7881.28
08-01	7889.24				7121.46
07-16	8694.71				7505.41
07-01	6958.47				6834.15
06-16	5770.92				5600.13
06-01	6276.35				5828.92
05-16	6422.87				6112.88
05-01	5334.33				5120.76
04-16	6083.76				5606.32
04-01	8214.48				7447.81
03-16	8774.58				7960.20
03-01	7064.87				6662.22
02-16	7031.79				6516.51
02-01	6860.00				6454.74
01-16	6609.36				6207.27
01-01	5144.41				4939.09
12-16	4986.44				4863.01

This is a report showing actual deposits I earned selling various information products on clickbank during a recent 18 month period. I have several clickbank accounts, but this is my strongest one.

3. A book can live much longer now. It doesn't have to expire.

Another great benefit of writing eBooks is that you can easily update the product at any point, and if you so choose, you can reward your past readers with a brand-new copy for free. When's the last time that happened to you as a reader? I've done it numerous times with my eBooks. I collect the email addresses of my readers when they buy, and then send them free updates for life. There are readers of this very book who have devoured all seven previous versions of it, but they paid only once.

4. Very often an eBook is better than a "real book."

Some are surprised to hear that I'd rather sell an eBook to someone than a "real book" in nearly all cases. There are several reasons for this, not the least of which is the amount of money that I earn. The book you are now reading had a lot of people touching it before it actually got to you. Everyone gets their piece of the pie including the paper company, the ink company, the glue in the binding company, the printing press business, the marketers, the publishers, the guy who sweeps the publisher's floor at two in the morning, etc. What does that leave me with in the end? Not much.

With an eBook however, the delivery is instantaneous and free and my profit margins are huge in comparison. That's not the best part of the story, though. The best part is when someone buys an eBook from me I get their email address. This means I can follow-up with them and give them current updates, other products and services of interest, and I can begin to build a lifelong relationship with that customer.

Another benefit of an eBook is that I can interact more with the customer. I can include clickable links inside that take readers to blog posts, articles or other supporting content online. I can even sell something from inside the book, and a click or two later, the customer has the product ordered and I have been paid.

You can see why I'm such a huge fan of eBooks. It probably also makes sense now why I decided to write eBooks for 10 years before I ever had a "real book" published.

If you'd like a comprehensive course on writing a great book and promoting it correctly you should check out this course:

ProvenSelfPublishing.com

Choose good titles for your content

One of the great lessons that I learned a little late in my business career is the importance of the titles that I choose to use for my information products and content.

For any information or content that you create, take great care when giving it a name. The name or title of your content is the first impression, and you will gain or lose many readers or viewers based on what you decide to call it.

For example, most professional copywriters will tell you that they spend as much if not more time on the title or header of a sales letter than they do on the rest of the entire document. You can assign a lot of value to your content and information if you use powerful words to title it and describe it.

As you begin creating a steady flow of content keep in mind that the titles you choose are a significant factor in how much impact your efforts will have.

Great titles give the content a feel of "exclusivity" and "simplicity" at the same time. Creating top 10 lists, or step-by-step lists make for great content.

EXAMPLES:

- Seven things every puppy owner must know about housebreaking

- Five back pain secrets your doctor won't tell you

- Special report: Getting out of debt step-by-step

- Eight steps to landing your dream job fast

You'll notice that I failed to follow my own advice in choosing a title for this book! The simple explanation is the fact that I wrote this book very early in my career and it took off in spite of my poor choice of title. Now that the term "silent sales machine" has been branded and associated with being a great book, I'd be crazy to abandon the title.

If I had it to do all over again however, I probably would have chosen a much more descriptive title such as, "The three online strategies that have earned me millions online."

As a reminder—I talked a lot in Chapter 3 about other content creation strategies (email, video, etc.).

Start creating content!

If you aren't an expert, just interview one!

Everyone enjoys being considered an expert by their peers. Use this universal truth to your advantage. Most experts in any field will readily agree to being interviewed by an engaging fellow expert with a win-win proposition.

Some of the easiest and most potent content that you can ever deliver to your audience will simply be interviews with relevant experts.

If you find yourself having trouble getting the attention of the higher-level experts in your field, then I suggest you use what I call "the bottom up" approach. When using "the bottom up" approach to securing experts, you start out by contacting the least influential and most eager experts in your field of interest. For example, these are the authors who appear well beyond page one on Amazon or Google. These experts aren't hard to find and typically they are more than willing to volunteer the information they know in a telephone interview regardless of your marketing power or intentions. Once you've approached and interviewed several of the lesser known experts, you can begin to approach the more influential experts with a bit more credibility and experience and you'll find that most of them will be far more likely to agree to an interview if you've already interviewed people who they consider to be their peers. Of course you will have gotten testimonials from each of them as well!

More influential experts may be interested in knowing what your marketing plans are in exchange for their valuable ideas and time. The best answer you can give them is that you'll be exposing them to your large following. Ideally, this is a large email list, popular blog, or other popular forum.

What if you don't have an audience yourself yet to help convince the "big fish" that you are worth the effort?

The bottom up strategy still works. It may take slightly more effort, but when approaching experts who are lower on the totem pole you can suggest to them that you will provide them with a copy of your interview as well as a full transcript for their use in whatever way they see fit for their own audience. Inside the transcript that you create, you can include links back to your blog or better yet your email list. As your list grows so does your ability to attract the influential leaders in your niche.

As you work your way up the totem pole of influential people in your niche, you will find it easier and easier to get the time and attention of both the experts and the audiences that they are reaching. With each interview that you conduct, be sure to deliver the content of the interview in an attractive, professional format that the expert can easily share with their own audience. If you conduct a high energy, exciting, personal, and engaging interview, the expert will be more than delighted to share it with their audience. Most people will have no problem with you conservatively sprinkling in your contact information, your website, or details on joining your email list.

There are several free tools that you can use to accommodate such interviews. I've frequently used the services of FreeConferenceCall.com to conduct interviews by phone and then easily generate an MP3 or WAV file for easy distribution to my audience.

Transcription services can be used to turn any spoken recording into a written transcript. The services I use also are able to correct the grammar as they create the document because few of us speak in full sentences.

An attractive e-cover can easily be created as well using any number of eBook or e-cover services online.

Give the file, the transcript, and the attractive cover to every expert you interview and request that they give the product away as a download to their followers (or sell the product and keep the proceeds). Of course, inside of the product will be a handful of conservative references to you and instructions on joining your email list or getting more information from you.

Using "tele-seminar" services to record experts or train your audience

Tele-seminars are one of my favorite ways to capture amazing content and to communicate with an audience either live or with the recording of a call. A tele-seminar is nothing more than a recorded telephone conversation among two or more people. As soon as the call is over, you have an MP3 recording that can be edited or used as is. It can be transcribed and turned into a book if you so desire. It's instant, easy content.

Typically the tele-seminar is a presentation conducted by one or at most three or four *hosts*, while a large number of audience *participants* can listen in and in some cases, interact with the hosts. The only thing that distinguishes a host from a participant is control of the recording and mute features of the call.

The only thing you need is a free account with FreeConferenceCall.com, Skype.com or any other similar service. If using Skpe just do a Google search for a reputable call recorder. Don't us a free version or you'll be limited to short calls.

You could host a tele-seminar five minutes from now, if you wanted to. They don't have to be scheduled—all you need is two or more people on the phone and then press the record button.

On many occasions, I've arranged to interview or discuss interesting topics with an expert in my industry by way of a simple tele-seminar call. Sometimes I'll invite a live audience to listen in as well by sharing a specific date and time with my audience so they can join in and listen.

If I have a live audience I can mute and un-mute them as the host for a question-and-answer session while recording the entire event. With more than a handful of people on the line at a time, the background noise can easily get out of hand, so the primary host needs to be ready to mute out all participants whenever necessary. Individual participants can also mute themselves so that only those with questions can be heard and recorded. With more than 10 people or so on the line, the odds of background noise goes up dramatically unless you have control of the mute features of the service you are using.

I've conducted training courses where students paid thousands of dollars to receive the training and coaching I delivered, and the entire content of the course consisted of recorded tele-seminar sessions that were later transcribed into printable documents.

Some tips from a tele-seminar veteran:

- Always start out the call by introducing yourself briefly and then the expert/guest thoroughly. Give any guest expert recognition for whatever accomplishments or websites that they've told you (prior to the call) that they would like to have mentioned. Half way through and at the end of the call, remind your listeners who it is that they've been listening to, and also remind them briefly again of the book or website that your expert is hoping to "pitch."

- At the start of the call, briefly summarize the topics that you'll be covering in the order that you'll be covering them. Your listeners will appreciate that they can fast-forward to the points most interesting to them.

- Keep the energy level up by being excited about the topic and content. Your audience won't be more "into it" than you are.

- Try not to breathe into the headset and remind your other hosts of the same rule

- Make sure your other hosts make liberal use of the mute feature. If a barking dog or other interruption enters the scene on a host, it is their job to mute out.

- If any of the hosts seem to have a bad connection, have them immediately hang up and dial back in.

- Use a land line whenever possible—never a cell phone unless entirely unavoidable.

- Don't stick too closely to a script. Let the call flow freely.

- Two or more hosts is better than one. Each host should say something every few minutes. Don't let one person ramble on too long or it gets boring.

- Give participants a warning when you are about to ask questions so that they are ready for it—otherwise you'll have dead air when you "flip the mute switch" and invite them to join in.

- All hosts give each other permission to gently interrupt and occasionally talk over each other so that it sounds less scripted and more like a real conversation (picture the news commentary shows with guests . . . don't worry about "polite"). This type of banter is easy to listen to, but polite pauses between each speaker will make the audio seem to drag on.

- Make sure that you share these tips with the other call "hosts" well ahead of time.

- Shorter calls that "leave them wanting more" are always better than "longer" calls that end awkwardly and slowly.

- Tell everyone how to get more help if they need it.

- At more than one place in the call, announce who you are interviewing and what the content of the call is.

- Educate don't pitch.

- Consider having a "silent assistant" join you on the line as a host so that they can control the mute/unmute features of the participants as well as the recording start and stop feature. On a large call with many participants, it's nice to have someone greet people as they show up on the call (unmuted) and ask their names and where they are from as well as introduce the main hosts when you are ready to begin. Another responsibility that this silent assistant can perform is to monitor an email account where questions can be submitted in real time for the presenters to answer as they come in. The assistant can pass the "good" questions to the presenters, and answer the less "broadcast worthy" questions individually.

- Don't let the call go longer than 45 minutes to an hour. Schedule a second call if necessary.

- Provide the expert with a handful of questions before the interview begins and allow the expert to add in their own questions as well. Don't spend too much time scripting the interview, though—instead let it flow naturally as a conversation.

- For added value, create a list of time marks and topics covered in the audio and add that information near the download link for your interview. This makes the audio far more usable when posted on your blog or other website. See the chapter on podcasting for ideas on posting and sharing audio content.

While the above rules generally apply to recorded phone calls or Skype calls, most of the above rules also apply to "on camera" virtual meetings as well. Two options for on camera meetups are Spreecast.com and of course Google Hangouts.

It takes some practice to use these services effectively, but with them, you can learn to build incredible relationships with your audience and fellow experts as you meet online virtually.

Impromptu recordings

Have you ever been on the phone with someone and had such an interesting conversation that the two of you wound up wishing you had recorded the whole thing? Don't let this happen to you. You can sign up for a free account with any number of free conference call services in a matter of seconds.

Frequently when I have the opportunity to connect on the phone with someone interesting or passionate about any subject, I will ask them to dial into my FreeConferenceCall.com phone number or Skype so that we can easily record the conversation for future use. This is just one more creative way to capture quick content. I do this type of thing all the time and it costs me nothing to capture this amazing content.

Get your content out there . . . even if it's free!

This book is full of ideas and my goal is that it will inspire you to be a content creator, no matter what direction you go from here.

Here's an inspirational story from a friend of mine that will hopefully encourage you to take the simplest of ideas and share them for free with the world. Great things *will* happen when you take this step.

> **SUCCESS STORY:** From garage tinkering to celebrity status in the music industry!
>
> For several years my guitar playing buddy Brian and I worked on houses together fixing up junkers—using loans and investment money from our parents. He had serious construction skills. I mainly did "grunt" work.
>
> Neither of us enjoyed this type of work, but we were trying to supplement our income so that we could each work on our true passions online. Luckily for us we stopped buying houses and started focusing online!
>
> His true passion was guitars and more specifically, the tiny niche market of "guitar pedal mods" (if you've never heard of "guitar pedal mods" don't worry—it will all make sense in a minute). Working together on houses gave us time to talk . . . and those talks helped each of us establish what can now easily be considered "online empires."

The theme in many of our talks was the power of the word "free"—and it wound up working out great for both of us!

For years, bands in the Indianapolis, Indiana area all knew that there was a guy locally who was "the man" when it came to making a guitar pedal produce sounds way cooler than they were supposed to produce. Musicians call these guitar pedal "mods" and Brian was "the man."

Brian would tediously work weekends and evenings on one guitar pedal at a time for band buddies and local musician friends. He made a decent side income charging for his services, but he was "trading a few dollars for a few hours" and neither of us would ever settle for that.

As my Internet career began to take off slightly ahead of his, Brian and I had several conversations about how he could use his unique skill to grow a real business around his passion driven niche. I was sold on the "free content" concept as his best approach.

The "free content" concept:

Brian began taking digital pictures and documenting the process he used to modify various guitar pedals and turn them into the valuable "mods" that his local fans were enjoying. He turned these "digital courses" into PDF files that could be easily downloaded or printed and mailed to his increasingly eager fan base. Inevitably, each course that he produced and distributed would lead to more questions, more followers, and more fans of what he was trying to do. The more he distributed this free and inexpensive content online, the more his fan base grew. The demand for his guitar pedal "mods" and manuals and other related instructional material began to steadily increase to the point where he had to hire help to meet demand.

Although I'm sure Brian isn't the only guy in the world that can crack open a guitar pedal and modify it with a soldering tool, I am sure he's the only one who took the time to document the process and then give the information away in order to grow a raving fan base of people who "get it."

His reward?

Dozens of the top musicians in the world now use and rave about "Wampler Pedals." He has his own brand on store shelves around the world, and has worked with some of the most talented musicians on the planet that now rave about his custom equipment. At music equipment conventions he spends the entire weekend signing autographs for eager fans.

You can now get the full story at WamplerPedals.com and see where Brian's passion and the word "free" have taken him lately. The last time I checked Brad Paisley, Keith Urban, Brent Mason, Skillet and dozens of other world recognized artists were using Brian's stuff.

4.2 Using eBay as a Silent Sales Machine

In previous versions of this book I spent a good deal of time teaching readers how to see eBay not merely as a place to "sell stuff," but also as a place to establish yourself as an expert and to grow an audience. This story sums up how one reader took my advice to heart and built an empire:

> We started Liberty Jane Clothing on eBay a couple of years ago. My wife was truly great at making 18 inch doll clothes, so we quickly found a following.
>
> Twelve months later we were PowerSellers, and making around $1,000 per month. One month we excitedly topped $1,500. The problem was that we had reached the limit of our business model, (which consisted of sewing outfits one at a time, and listing them on eBay one at a time). Although we were happy to be making some nice side money, she was burned out, so we really needed to figure out a new approach.
>
> Unfortunately our operation just wasn't sustainable, or scaleable. We needed to figure out how to leverage her unique skill, while freeing up her time. We had already decided that making mass manufactured items, or selling other peoples' mass manufactured

items, wasn't right for us. Hiring people didn't seem right for us either. We felt stuck.

Then we got your book "The Silent Sales Machine." The message was clear—build an email list, and offer digital products to your customers.

The entire next summer we debated publishing my wife's patterns as PDF guidebooks. We knew we could do it, but worried about whether it was the right business strategy. It felt like a huge gamble.

Would we be creating an army of competitors all using her patterns to undermine her auction prices?

Would other people take her work and go further than we'd been able to up to that point?

Finally that fall we decided to trust Jim's advice, and go digital.

That month we set up a new site, LibertyJanePatterns.com, published a few patterns as PDF guidebooks, offered some for free, and ended the month having sold 11. It was the start of a new product category for us that had one huge benefit, it was easily scaleable.

Within six months, our pattern guidebooks category was making as much as our eBay auctions ever had, and the decision to offer digital products had proven to be a no-brainer. None of our fears materialized, and we've discovered more benefits than we could have imagined. Today we are adding over 100 people per week to our newsletter list, and last month we had over 2,200 patterns downloaded. We have over 2,500 YouTube subscribers, and over 2,600 Facebook fans. Our business model today includes multiple digital products, downloads and coaching courses.

By allowing other seamstresses to use our patterns for sew-from-home businesses for free (we call them partners), we've actually created an interesting secondary market that hasn't diminished the value of our original outfits—instead it's actually enhanced them. In the near future we are working to overhaul our websites to accommodate the continued growth, and we're working on publishing two exciting new books which we know will be a hit with our customers.

Thanks for publishing the "Silent Sales Machine," Jim!

UPDATE TO THE STORY:

Jason and Cinnamon Miles (they are the ones who sent me the above letter) have now gone on to have tremendous success in the "self publishing" arena with their original books on not only doll related topics, but also social media and online marketing! I also partnered with them to create my first ever "self-publishing" course available at ProvenSelfPublishing.com

As eBay has matured as a marketplace, it has gotten more difficult to attract a niche audience there, but it can still be done! To stay up to date on the latest trends in using eBay and Amazon as a creative tool for expanding your audience, visit this blog post and contribute you ideas and observations:

http://www.jimcockrum.com/blog/2014/01/31/using-ebay-and-amazon-to-generate-leads-grow-your-audience/

> **HOT TIP:** Grow email lists in multiple niche markets using ONE eBay account.
>
> I created a YouTube video that shows you step by step how to grow multiple mailings lists automatically on eBay by inviting each of your eBay buyers to get on an email mailing list based on the product they purchased. Watch the video here:
>
> https://www.youtube.com/watch?v=FM165MxO9hc
>
> Examples of how this could work for you:
>
> - If you sell guitar picks on eBay, you can quickly grow an email list of people who play guitar.
>
> - If you sell dog treats on eBay, you can grow an audience of dog lovers.
>
> - If you sell any low ticket, impulse buy item that is purchased by enthusiasts of any niche, you can grow a great email list in any or all of those niche markets using the simple strategy in the above video.

Depending on the niche you are in, you could actually *lose* money on each eBay sale, but build an incredible list of customers for repeat and future purchases!

General eBay Tips to Maximize Exposure and Profits Regardless of Your Business Approach to eBay

When it comes to maximizing eBay profits, the basic principles are that the more *targeted* visitors who see your item for sale, and the better deal you are able to get on your inventory when sourcing it, the more likely you are to make a nice profit on the item.

Here are some facts to keep in mind to maximize your profits on eBay:

1. Hardly any eBay visitors search using auction descriptions!

Some eBay visitors do advanced searches on eBay and look at the detailed descriptions, of course—but the vast majority still use *title search only*.

> **ONE EXCEPTION:** The more obscure the item you're selling, the more likely it is people will search in titles *and* descriptions.

Knowing this, it is very important that you spend the time to write a *great* title. It must contain the keywords that your buyers are most likely to search for. Any other "fluff" words are entirely optional. Fill it up with words that shoppers are likely to use to find your listing. Save the descriptive words for the listing body, but don't take up space in your title with them.

If you absolutely must have non-keyword words, try to abbreviate them. Superlatives are a waste of space. Sure, you think the item you're selling is "beautiful" or "great" or "amazing" or "stunning" or "excellent" or whatever. But people *never* search for those words, and they don't seem to be that much of an enticement anyway. If you can't resist calling your product "Excellent", at least abbreviate it to "Exc" to make room for more keywords.

2. Shoppers tend to search "all of eBay," not categories

Although not as overwhelmingly lopsided as the "titles only" vs. "titles and descriptions" comparison mentioned in point one above, the majority of eBay users who search for items (as opposed to browsing) do so from eBay's home page or eBay's main Search box.

The next most commonly used search location is the one that appears in the left-hand column of auction listings.

But don't assume it's profitable or that it makes sense to be listed in extra categories if you're going to be lumped in a category with thousands of other sellers.

3. Auctions are going out of style, fixed price rules!

When eBay first came on the scene, auctions were *cool* and *fun*. Several years later, eBay shoppers are spoiled by the Amazon option, and they want to buy stuff *now* for the most part. Unless you have a truly unique item that is highly sought after by many potential bidders who are all ready for a bidding "war," I suggest you *always* assign a fixed price to your listings.

4. Ending day and time can make an enormous difference

Half of all eBay users live in the Eastern Time Zone. So while an auction that ends at 10 pm Pacific Time may seem okay if you live in California, the average Pennsylvanian, for example, will not be "eBaying" at 1 am.

That's pretty obvious to professional eBay sellers.

But what may be less obvious is that there are different "body clocks" associated with different items. Some of them make sense. For example, video games and accessories sell well at night. Office equipment and supplies sell well in the morning.

Day of the week is also enormously important.

There's an old eBay legend that says auctions that end on a Sunday night get more visitors. That may be true in some categories, but that's a gross generalization.

Until you actually do the analysis for the type of item(s) you sell, it's all guesswork, and there are no easy rules of thumb that are entirely universal.

Using a tool like Terapeak can help you figure out the optimal ending time for any product based on recent successful auctions of similar or identical items. This is just one of the many uses for this powerful research tool.

4.3 Amazon.com and FBA (Fulfillment by Amazon)

You are probably aware that eBay and Amazon are the online giants of online commerce.

In the previous section, I wrote about eBay. But there's an even bigger player in the game now and it's a truly international opportunity (no matter where you live in the world, you can do this business).

You can learn the basics of how to sell on Amazon by visiting Amazon.com and checking out the information on the "Sell on Amazon" page. The link to that page is located on the homepage of Amazon.com as of this writing. (Note: I'm not talking about *affiliate* marketing with Amazon in this chapter. I'm talking about selling physical products. But this business model *can* be hands free, as you'll soon see!)

The best selling course in the world on the topic of getting started on Amazon as a seller and doing it *right* is this course:

http://www.provenamazoncourse.com/

> **TESTIMONY:** One of hundreds of success stories about our Amazon course:
>
> I jumped in head first in October (with Jim's Amazon course). My sales grew gradually and last month (8 mos. later) I had over 16K in sales. I had replaced my *job* salary. Here I am today. I spend all day

with my kids and don't miss them growing up. I have a business I *love* and I'm so very proud of. I could not be happier and I have you to thank. My family is the most important thing in my life and I am able to be there to take my kids to school every single day. I really appreciate everything you do and the way you help people. You have helped me become a successful entrepreneur and an even better father.

Regards,
—Matt

See many more success stories at ProvenAmazonCourse.com

Here's a brief overview of eBay vs. Amazon as well as Amazon FBA.

In case you are unfamiliar with FBA, Amazon's FBA (Fulfillment by Amazon) is just what it sounds like. It's the shipping and order fulfillment side of Amazon. You can send any inventory you'd like to Amazon (even large items) and they will store and ship them to your customers when they sell—no matter what method you use to sell them. This means even some eBay sellers use Amazon fulfillment as their storage and shipping service.

Let's start out with some basic observations:

Advantages of selling on Amazon:

- Virtually any barcoded item can be easily sold on Amazon even if you put your own barcode on it.

- Biggest online shopping audience (recently one in five Internet users stopped by Amazon in a single month according to Mashable.com).

- If you don't want to box and ship every item yourself, you can send all your inventory to Amazon using their FBA program (advantages and disadvantages of FBA discussed below).

Disadvantages of Amazon:

- It's impossible to capture customer email addresses & Amazon is *very* protective of this. They consider your buyer to be *their* customers . . . not yours.

- Some categories on Amazon require approval and/or experienced sellers only.

- Keeping track of your fees and total expenses can be tricky. Watch the numbers!

- Everything is a commodity on Amazon. It's hard to set yourself apart in some categories.

When to use eBay instead of Amazon:

- When selling any unique, old, collectible, or other unusual item, it's best to use eBay.

- If you are trying to grow a list of customers using creative marketing, it's only likely to happen on eBay.

- If you are making a profit! (test *anything*)

- For exposure of your idea or brand or information.

- If you want to diversify, use both!

Disadvantages of eBay (compared to Amazon):

- Seemingly conflicting and constantly shifting rules.

- Not quite as much traffic as Amazon.com.

- You ship every item yourself (unless you use Amazon's FBA).

- You can't take a vacation without shutting down your business.

FBA is simply Amazon's fulfillment service. This means they offer to do the storage and shipping for you if you choose to let them. There are numerous advantages to going this route and a few disadvantages as well. Here's my list:

Advantages of adding Amazon FBA service to your business:

- Grow as large as you'd like without having to hire much (or any) help to ship your various products to customers worldwide. You can go virtually hands free and create a "Silent Sales Machine" this way.

- Sell *anything*. Be as diverse as you'd like in your inventory selections without worrying about all the headaches that go with being "diversified."

- Take a vacation anytime you'd like and your business continues to function—unlike eBay where each box is shipped by you.

- Purge old inventory with the click of a button (they will destroy/donate it for you).

- Cheap storage.

- Simplify your business model. You are in the business of doing *one thing*: finding profitable inventory (no more customers to deal with!)

- Fast, reliable and *very* cheap shipping for your customers.

- If you choose to list your items in the Amazon marketplace (you don't have to) your products are listed as "Fulfilled by Amazon" giving you a huge advantage—especially to those millions of shoppers with "Amazon Prime" memberships (they get free shipping on FBA items they order).

- If you choose to sell the items yourself using eBay, your own website, or any other method, Amazon FBA can still be your fulfillment agent (but you are crazy not to *also* list your items on Amazon.com to see what happens).

- Your listings on Amazon are more likely to appear on top of the page when searches are performed by shoppers. This is because Amazon would rather ship from their own warehouse than rely on shippers that are shipping their goods from home or various businesses.

- Amazon handles all return issues for you. Like I said before—no customer hassles.

Disadvantages of FBA:

- Storage fees can sneak up on you if you don't purge your inventory (Amazon offers a free inventory report to show you what products they suggest you purge to avoid higher fees.) Overall the fees are *very cheap*.

- Loss of physical control of your inventory.

- Difficulty tracking fees.

- Only works for barcoded items. Doesn't work for collectibles, unique one of a kind items, etc. You *can* however add your "commodity"—like items into the Amazon inventory as long as you first secure a bar code for the item. The ProvenAmazonCourse mentioned above can help with that.

We get many great success stories about our Amazon FBA training. Here are some recent examples:

TESTIMONY: Hi Jim—I'm *killing* it on Amazon thanks to *your* ProvenAmazonCourse.com advice . . . (My 'Units Sold' and 'profit per unit' have *skyrocketed*. My ROI is upwards of 300% net of commission/shipping/fba fees/pro merchant subscriptions, etc. My *5-star 100% perfect customer rating along with a "1.00" perfect internal account score* have given me the ability to work from home *full time* (I have a part time weekend only job too). To scale my biz, *every single cent* earned on Amazon using the FBA platform gets reinvested into more/more/more inventory. Positioned beautifully for the upcoming holiday season.

—S. Friedman

TESTIMONY: My monthly average the last few months was $38,000. Don't know my GP yet, waiting on my accountant, but the bills are paid. I have 4 staff and the total weekly hours is about 180. I plan on exceeding $600,000 this year. Jim, your course was the first step I took when I decided to do Amazon, and I definitely benefited greatly, as I have told countless people over the last year (I started exactly one year ago). Just this morning, I made a comment when someone asked if the ProvenAmazonCourse.com course was of value on a Yahoo discussion forum. If you want to know how I went from nothing but the PAC to $40,000+/month, I would be happy to speak with you.

—R. Prince

TESTIMONY: Let me start by saying I sincerely wish I had known about this amazing program when I started researching work at home options a few years ago. The Proven Amazon Course and the JimCockrumCoaching.com program are nothing short of outstanding! There is absolutely no limit to how far you can grow this business if you are willing to put forth the effort and take massive action on what you learn. The business model is simply brilliant! It's not a difficult business to learn and operate and it actually becomes quite addictive when you really get it going! My advice for anyone looking to start a business from home is to purchase the Proven Amazon Course *today* and get involved with the wonderful people over at Jim Cockrum Coaching! Do what they say, work consistently, and you will succeed with this wonderful program!

—Tommy L.

For dozens more success stories visit ProvenAmazonCourse.com

What will sell well on Amazon?

Spend some time browsing Amazon.com. You'll discover millions of products are being sold there. Everything from diapers to pool tables. Amazon relies on third party sellers like us to stock their warehouses and their website with millions of products, but the best part is we have the option of letting Amazon warehouse and ship the product for us (this option is called FBA or Fulfillment By Amazon). This means no matter where you live in the world, you can sell just about anything on Amazon into any country where they have warehouses.

Some tips on what to sell on Amazon no matter where you live in the world

NOTE: If you live outside the U.S., scroll to the end of this section for a U.S. based business that will label and ship your inventory to Amazon for you!

Bulk wholesale

If you are wiling to do a bit of research there are unlimited opportunities to buy bulk and flip the inventory over to Amazon.

http://www.mysilentteam.com/public/Real-Wholesale-Sources.cfm

Trade Show inventory (without leaving home)

Attending trade shows is a great way to find eager manufacturers ready to sell you inventory at great prices. This simple book will teach you all you need to know about tapping into this fantastic inventory strategy:

TradeShowNoShow.com

Buy anything seasonal once it goes on sale and hold it for 9-10 months & sell it for *huge* profits

Seasonally hot items that are purchased off season are a great bet! Buying any seasonal specific items right when they go on sale after a major holiday is almost always a sure fire profitable item on Amazon 10 months later.

TESTIMONY: Last year (before attending Jim's CES conference) I didn't think people bought Valentine's Day items online, but this year we sold $10,535 in Valentine's day sales in just last 30 days!

—L. Wolf

Retail arbitrage

When shopping in retail outlets you can easily scan the barcode of any item with a smartphone and see what the item is selling for on Amazon. We have hundreds of students who make a full time living after taking our course, and this is the *only* strategy they use to earn tens of thousands monthly on Amazon.

How can I make good inventory buying decisions?

Learning the proper strategy for making good inventory buying decisions is very important. We have a saying that we use all the time around here—it's this: *"You make your money when you buy your inventory, not when you sell it."* This means you should do your hard work and research *before* you buy inventory. Once you buy into your inventory, it's really hard to "push it" if the market doesn't want it. In other words, only buy stuff that you have a great deal of certainty about.

While just about anyone can see an obviously good inventory deal, it takes a trained eye to spot a good lower margin deal that is worth pursuing. For example, if you see a popular widget being sold locally "off the shelf" of a local retailer for $20 and it's selling consistently for $100 on Amazon, then common sense tells you it's worth scooping up as many as you can get. However, if you are considering buying 500 "widgets" for $20 that are currently selling on Amazon for $45, but that same product has a history of going up and down in price with multiple other sellers competing with you, then you'll need to be well aware of the potential risks when making your decision.

Some tools that can be helpful when making inventory buying decisions:

Sales rank

On Amazon, the product sales rank is easily accessed by looking up any product. This info is useful, but keep in mind that a "high" sales rank is not a guarantee of sales results, nor is a "low" sales rank an indication that you shouldn't pursue a particular item. Sales rank is subject to major fluctuation from day to day for many lower ranked products as well. Use the below helpful graph to help gauge what the sales rank might mean for any given product:

http://www.mysilentteam.com/public/Amazon-Categories-Decision-Helper.cfm

Recent eBay results tell a story too.

If a product is selling well on eBay, it's quite likely to sell well on Amazon too. Use the recent pricing levels on eBay to get an idea of what the online value of an item is currently. To search recent sales on eBay use the "advanced" search feature and search "completed" listings.

> **TIP:** *Live outside the U.S.?* Or *need help labeling your product?*
>
> Would you like to have someone else help you with labeling your product and sending it to Amazon.com? Especially if you live outside of the U.S., you'll need a partner inside the U.S. who can help with this task so you can avoid shipping your inventory twice before it gets to Amazon. Check out this service:
>
> http://forms.aweber.com/form/72/642801472.htm
>
> This video will be helpful as well in answering some of your questions:
>
> http://youtu.be/z3aHz1gNZrI

More ideas for finding Profitable Inventory to Sell on eBay (or Amazon)

If you are out shopping and encounter an item that you think might sell well online, it's pretty easy to do a quick check on eBay or Amazon with any smart phone.

There are also several great online sites and services to use to find hot inventory.

If any item has a significantly higher price on Amazon as compared to the store you are visiting, and IF it is likely to sell within a few months (a decent sales rank) then you've found a winner. I shoot for 200–300% profits so that all fees and other expenses are easily covered.

Virtually every time I visit a retail store, I come across winning items to add to my FBA inventory. The closeout aisle of any major chain store will have great finds on it most of time as will any overstock discount store. Take along a smartphone for easy Amazon price checks with a quick barcode scanner (there are multiple free and fee based barcode scanners that can be added as an app to any smartphone).

Can you automate your inventory search?

I pay workers locally to help run my entire eBay and Amazon business. As of this writing, one of the hired workers is my mom! I share profits with them as incentive to help grow my business. When we hire anyone, we ask them to sign a non-compete agreement with us and they are barred from selling on eBay or Amazon themselves so that I can freely share tips and ideas with them without risk of creating well armed local competitors. Once you are ramped up and ready to pursue other income options, this is a great way to automate your business so you can set about creating multiple income streams.

Ready to learn Amazon from the best teachers in the biz (including me?)

Recently I recruited about 12 of the top sellers on Amazon and Amazon FBA selling and we put together a training course that is by far the best you'll find anywhere. I say this with confidence because all of the experts also contribute to our discussion forum. If you want to hang out with other FBA and Amazon sellers and get your questions answered by pros then consider the full training course at ProvenAmazonCourse.com.

Concluding thoughts for Chapter 4

If the *only* chapter of this book that you read is this one and IF you take action based on what you've just ready, you'll be in great shape launching income streams online. This chapter is easily a book all by itself.

One thought you might be having at this point is, "This sounds like work." You are right—it is work, but it's the most rewarding work I've ever known. In the next chapter I'll reveal some of the bad ideas you might have had pushed at you as you've been searching for ideas online. I'll do my best to share my 10 years of experience with you, then it's up to you to take action.

CHAPTER 5

Where You Should NOT Start

Have you noticed that all of the experts who are selling "how to make money online" courses all seem to flash big checks and big results in an effort to impress you?

Do you ever feel like you are only getting part of the story? Do you keep seeing the same people endorsing each other's stuff over and over again?

Do you ever ask yourself questions like this:

"If guru X has tens of thousands of followers and hundreds of them are taking his courses, then where are the hundreds of success stories?"

The truth is, you *are* only getting part of the story and you *should* be asking questions like that!

Allow me to illustrate.

Check out the below picture of one of my sons and I—it's an unedited picture, and a very *real* picture. It makes me look like a champ doesn't it? Sure it's "true", but **you aren't getting the whole story** as you'll soon see. I put this pic in here to make a very important point, and the lesson will soon be clear to you.

I'll reveal the lesson of this picture at the end of this chapter.

If you feel "new" to the idea of having an online business I have some proven advice from my decade of success (and over 15 years of "trying" to succeed).

I'll be revealing some pretty popular business models that are all bad ideas! These are the places you **should not start** no matter how big and flashy the pitch that tries to convince you otherwise.

This is my "*sucker list.*" It's the stuff newbies almost always fall for thinking they can pay someone to make them a success story. I'll explain my sucker list in more detail below, but here are some things to entirely avoid when you are first starting out (in my opinion):

- Pay Per Click Advertising (Google AdWords, Facebook ads, etc.)

- Search Engine Optimization (SEO)

- Affiliate Marketing (Selling other people's stuff for a commission)

- Building any kind of website (including simple blogs)

- Driving Traffic Gimmicks

- Virtually *everything* and *anything* "step-by-step" or "push button simple"

- Eagerly following a celebrity "guru"

- Big ticket coaching that won't give you access to the "main man" or other students that have taken the big ticket coaching (Insight: With my coaching you get access to not only me, but also all of my current and past students in a wide open forum.)

Millions of very smart and well intentioned people have spent (wasted) billions of dollars on the above activities because they were fooled into thinking that it was far easier than it really is.

Online business is *business* . . . and business is never "easy."

It can be fun, rewarding, challenging, entertaining, energizing, rewarding and fulfilling, but never "easy."

Until you feel very grounded, confident, and *creative* (I'll explain that later), then you should avoid all of the above "opportunities" and pursuits. Your odds of success *even with training* are abysmal.

I'm probably the *only* guy you'll ever hear this from, so call me crazy if you want to, but the fact is—*the statistics back me up*.

The facts are clear on this point.

FOLLOW THE HERD AND YOU'LL GET SLAUGHTERED

If you buy into *any* popular "Step by Step" course of any kind you'll wind up completing a bunch of steps that make you feel good (and yes, you might pick up some new useless skills or even have a shiny new website to show for it), but unless you are in the lucky 2%, you won't make any money. I'm sorry, but it's a sad truth that I've seen playing out for over a decade online.

There are some very popular personalities online with large followings, but nearly all of them lack one thing in my opinion. This glaringly obvious flaw in their "fame" of course is a significant number of true success stories (a raving *fan* is *not* the same thing as a success story). Among their supposed tens of thousands of raving fans and followers are there *really* only a handful making money?! They show only a handful of success stories on their website (and sure there are loads of people who "love" them and write great reviews because they think their guy is "cool" or "helpful" or "kind" or whatever), but in the end you just don't see a whole lot of people making any money.

These experts (well intentioned in many cases, perhaps) are simply good at making people feel good for the most part. Often times it's all masked in "step-by-step" courses that teach you to make money online while building your confidence that you are "doing something." They preach the "just do it" and "take action" religion.

They are masters of getting you to "invest in yourself" (a.k.a. give them a lot of money).

It's true in life and it's true online. Whatever the most popular leaders are teaching to the biggest crowds at any given time is probably total garbage or it will be very soon. It's been true forever in business.

Business success has always (and always will) belong to the creative mavericks.

Am I saying there are no systems to learn and apply? Of course not.

I *am* saying that the truly successful people who I'm working with (as well as the 2% of "followers" from my above example who are actually making some decent money) all have at least a few things in common. They posses some or all of the following characteristics and abilities:

- They watch what leaders do instead of just following leaders blindly.

- They don't "buy course after course"—they also watch how courses are sold and learn to sell.

- They don't follow the crowd, they find ways to build a crowd and then they sell their own ideas to the crowd.

- They apply successful concepts from two seemingly unrelated fields and combine them creatively.

- They know how to leverage and build *real* relationship online with other influential people.

- They know that success takes *time*. It never comes over night because of a course you bought yesterday.

For example, a true online pro might take a course from "Expert A" and then read a book by "Expert B" and then combine ideas from both experts into a brand new idea that they pursue themselves and it's unlike anything anyone else is doing. Then they teach this new strategy to others after they've succeeded themselves.

Confession time . . .

I'm in the business of teaching people how to make money online.

{GASP!}

That puts me in the company of some pretty slick scam artists. I've managed to keep my integrity and *not* "sell out," though. Sadly, I cannot say the same for many (most?) of my colleagues in this business.

What do I mean by "sell out"? In this business you "sell out" when you start promoting products (your own or those from someone else) that bring you a nice profit without any regard to the actual usefulness of the product or success rate that your audience can expect.

The most offensive (and hardest to detect) scam courses are those that make people "feel good" initially because they are so "step by step" helpful, full of great video, engaging and entertaining, but in the end all you have is a pretty website with links all over it and you start down the road of "driving traffic" or trying to find visitors for your new pretty site in a niche you could care less about. This "scam" approach has been done a thousand times—and surprisingly nearly every time a new "guru" comes on the scene and tries it, they get rich (while actually helping very few people).

It works because *you*—as the "student" will most likely blame yourself for the time-sucking failure, but as long as enough time has passed between "purchase point" and "frustration point" so that you don't ask for a refund, the "guru" that sold you the course wins and you'll wind up thinking that you are at fault. In my office we talk to people nearly every day that have been down that road—in some cases multiple times.

Success online is not a matter of step-by-step formulas or buying the right training courses from the right guru. I could make a *bunch* of money putting together such videos and courses, if I wanted to, because that's what people want in general. Don't be a sheep.

To further illustrate, here's a sarcastic article I wrote on this topic that shows how to be a rich Internet Marketing Guru in four simple steps:

http://www.jimcockrum.com/blog/?p=944

If that doesn't set you straight, nothing will. Please put this book down, go find a popular, even likeable "expert" and go try their system out for six months. Come back to this book (put it on your calendar) after you've failed to make any money (because you will in all likelihood fail, just like the other 98% of those who followed the herd to slaughter).

What about that sucker list I talked about earlier?

I told you to avoid these activities if you are new to online business. That means *until you are making or growing a following online you should keep away from all of the following activities:*

1. Pay Per Click Advertising

2. Search Engine Optimization (SEO)

3. Affiliate Marketing (it's just the "gravy on the top"—it's not an online income strategy all by itself)

4. Building any kind of website (including simple blogs)

5. Driving Traffic Strategies

6. Virtually *everything* "step-by-step" or "push button simple"

7. Eagerly following a celebrity "guru"

I'll go through this list one at a time in a moment, but your level of success and frustration both rely heavily on you trusting me here.

If you are considering buying a course, taking coaching, joining a membership site, or attending a conference that promises to help you in any of the above areas, the odds are that you are *not ready to* get into those topics unless and until you are *actively already making money or growing a loyal following online.*

5.1 Pay Per Click (PPC)

Pay Per Click (PPC) is cutthroat for all popular niche markets. I'm talking about Facebook ads, Google AdWords, etc. It's a game being won by mathematics, big budgets, experience and total commitment to testing. There are also *millions* of "stupid dollars" being thrown in the mix constantly by newbies. This only drives up prices making it more difficult for anyone who isn't *super serious* about studying the process deeply. PPC and paid ads are *not* for newbies.

5.2 Search Engine Optimization (SEO)

Search Engine Optimization (SEO) is an entire industry that many people become mesmerized by and then are lured into a wild goose chase that nearly always ends badly.

If you want to skip this section and instead read my thoughts on "SEO" expressed in about 20 seconds, check out one of my shortest blog posts ever here:

http://www.jimcockrum.com/blog/2011/08/30/how-to-rank-high-on-google-long-term/

While there are several search engines that arguably could be included in this discussion, I'll only be referring to Google because all other search engines wish they were Google and are doing their best to emulate them. If anyone ever does pass Google, these same ideas will apply to them as well, I assure you.

While there is an entire industry set up to provide Search Engine Optimization (SEO) services to help businesses and websites get ranked on online search engines like Google, there are precious few honest experts who will tell you that there is absolutely no way you can ever be assured of a good ranking online. If anyone *promises* results in the short or long term, you should *run away*. Even if you are fortunate enough to "get ranked" well on Google in the short term, the odds are against you being there long term unless you are both *fortunate and focused* in your efforts to maintain your rank using *legitimate* strategies which I'll explain in a moment.

I've encountered countless website owners who could have sworn they had cracked the Google code, but inevitably they've all realized a harsh reality (or soon likely will). Google is too smart to be fooled long-term. Only quality sites that meet the Google standards will be rewarded. Anyone can go from page 1 on Google to page 431 overnight. Pretending that this could never happen to you is simply inviting disaster. *I've chosen not to rely on my Google rankings as a result,* and neither should you in my opinion.

All of that being said, you should still pay attention to doing your best to generate the greatest amount of free traffic from Google that you possibly can.

What should you focus on in order to be rewarded by Google?

There are only two proven ways to get more "Google love":

> A. Have a great site with current, user friendly, keyword relevant information, and more importantly . . .

> B. Increase the number of quality pages that link to you.

In Google's own words: "Pages that we believe are important pages receive a higher PageRank and are more likely to appear at the top of the search results. Webmasters can improve the rank of their sites by *increasing the number of high-quality sites* that link to their pages."

What is this "PageRank"?

The "PageRank" metric used by Google is assigned to virtually every publicly accessible page online. You can measure the level of importance that Google assigns to any page by checking its page rank (PR). The score is a publicly viewable number from 0-10 with sites having a score of 0 or 1. You can easily add a Google "PageRank" indicator to your browser button bar and begin noticing the difference between sites that Google likes and sites that they barely even notice.

It has nothing to do with how "slick" or pretty the site is. It has everything to do with protecting the user experience when Google users enter a search phrase. Google wants the best of the best websites at the top. The best information, most up to date, most "linked to," etc.

WHAT'S THE DIFFERENCE BETWEEN "ORGANIC RESULTS" AND "PAID RESULTS"?

Keep In mind that this entire section is referring to Google's "organic results." These are the websites that Google likes and rewards with a good search engine rank at no expense whatsoever to the site owner. You'll notice when using the Google search engine that they always list the paid results or "Pay Per Click" ads down the right-hand side of the screen, as well as a handful of them at the top of the screen. All of these ads appear as a result of someone paying (in some cases, paying a lot) to appear in those positions. There are entire books written about the expensive prospect of effectively using these ads for advertising. I don't rely on "Pay Per Click" ads, and this book won't be discussing them very much at all because the learning curve is typically expensive when using them. In my opinion it's getting more and more difficult all the time to have success with PPC ads long-term.

Get more information on Google PR by searching Google for the term "page rank." Your efforts at increasing your level of respect from Google can easily be tracked by watching your score slowly creep up over time.

How does Google's algorithm really work?

To truly understand what you are up against when trying to "win the affections" of Google, you'll need to start to grasp how seriously they take the business of ranking websites. One of their core missions is to automate as much as possible the process of providing easy access to the best content on the Internet for all users of Google.com. Once you understand that core service as their goal, consider the fact that they've spent countless hours and millions of dollars hiring the most brilliant statisticians, mathematicians, genius level data analysts, etc., all chartered with the mission of creating a top-secret algorithm that automatically tracks and assigns page rank scores to every website online. They do all this to decide which sites will appear on which pages of the organic search results.

Yes—it's that complicated.

Want it all broken down in simple terms?

One of the best explanations I've ever heard of the Google ranking algorithm was as follows:

Imagine a large wall covered with light switches. There are rows and rows each with hundreds of light switches. Several top secret, genius level engineers are assigned the task of continually adjusting those light switches in such a way that the Google search engine performs at an optimum level. It is an ongoing process that never "stabilizes." The process never stabilizes because Google does not want anyone to know the exact nature of their algorithm. They don't want anyone to be able to manipulate their "machine." I even have a theory (it's my opinion, but I've met many other industry experts that wholeheartedly agree) that there are several random elements in this process that make it impossible to fully map it out by anyone . . . ever (even their own engineers).

The next time someone tells you that they can guarantee you results on Google, imagine that person matching wits with the multi-million dollar genius level process I've just described. While there is a chance that they might be able to accomplish some results some of the time short-term, the only long-term strategy that might work long-term is to "play by the rules." *This means creating unique quality content that multiple other quality websites will willingly (and voluntarily) link to.* The process of having other sites link to yours is called creating "back links." If anyone tells you that they can automate the process of creating great back links, you should know that they are participating in a process that Google is actively spending millions of dollars and many genius-level man hours trying to punish and eliminate. Again, it's worth repeating: *Google cannot be fooled long term. They will find the best websites and reward them, and they will find the sites that have automated the manipulation of their system and they will punish them. Google's own success hinges on their ability to do this task better than anyone else in the world, and they have the resources to do so!*

I have several sites that rank very well on Google for top keywords, but I've *never* (not even for ten minutes) focused on SEO strategies. That's right, I've never hired an SEO firm, and I don't read "driving traffic" books and tips. All I do is create great content that others want to get. The most work I do is finding potential partners who already have an audience that might want what I have to offer. This is the winning strategy that can't be stopped by Google or anyone else, for that matter.

To stay up to date on my thoughts regarding SEO visit my blog at JimCockrum.com and look for the SEO department.

> **TESTIMONY:** I've helped thousands of readers wake up to the realities of SEO. Here's one such letter we got:
>
> Jim—I now lean toward your thinking on the topic of SEO. It may be because SEO is still a mystery to me—"smoke & mirrors" maybe? So, I adopted two key strategies to build my online business:
>
> 1. Email strategy and
>
> 2. Build my subscriber base to ensure recurring revenues.
>
> These two approaches have allowed me to jack my job, so I now work full-time on my online business. The journey started when I picked up this book (SilentSalesMachine) when it became more obvious to me that if I viewed eBay as one of the best marketing tools out there I could attract more customers to my online shops

(not just my eBay shop). The model seems to work great, and without having to get involved in the SEO games.

—Gareth

5.3 Affiliate Marketing

"Affiliate marketing is a nice 'gravy on top' income model, but it is not a steady income business model for anyone except the most advanced experts—and with over a decade of experience, I'm still not one of them!" —Jim Cockrum

Affiliate marketing *is not* a viable business model.

There—I said it.

Rather than re-type out my thoughts on affiliate marketing, I think I'll refer you to my blog to educate you on what is possibly my most controversial (but nonetheless statistically *very true*) stance I take in this book. The sucker list *definitely* needs this topic on it!

Until you are *growing an audience* or *creating your own products* and making money in other creative ways, you should *never* get into "affiliate marketing." Your odds of success used to be decent, but now they are simply abysmal.

Here are some articles that will give you several reasons why a "newbie" should *never* get into affiliate marketing, and some good conversation from my readers about other options (be sure to join the conversation on any of these topics):

http://www.jimcockrum.com/blog/?p=1073
http://www.jimcockrum.com/blog/category/categories/grow-your-business/affiliate-marketing/
http://www.jimcockrum.com/blog/?p=1101
http://www.jimcockrum.com/blog/?p=1200

The "experts" love to teach affiliate marketing strategies because it's really not all that hard to get people excited about it, flash some big checks, get some tiny results for some people, and then supply a steady stream of "tips" to keep the crowd listening . . . but the dirty little secret is this: *"The **vast majority** (I'm talking 95% or so) of the people trying to make affiliate income aren't making more than a few bucks per week even after months or years of trying."* By the time someone gets that vested in the game, they tend to feel good about the "skills" that they've picked up along the way, but they are on a path to nowhere without some creative intervention.

I've attended conferences specifically aimed at affiliate marketers and they are depressing to me. These events are aimed at allowing the "best of the best" affiliate marketers to get together and share ideas, etc. Inevitably though, these conferences are *full* of people who have been trying for years to get that supposed "low hanging fruit" that is affiliate marketing income. It lures so many in—but the vast majority never achieve any significant results. When I've attended these events, my estimation is that 95% of the crowd is either selling something or struggling to find a way to finally make some money. It's not a place for "newbies"!

If you are someone who has been trying to generate affiliate income for a long time without success I suggest you check out the "Offline" chapter. You are more than ready to start helping real world businesses with the skills you've developed!

5.4 Building Any Kind of Website

Building any kind of website as your starting point in online business is a *huge* mistake.

I'm going against the grain of what you'll hear from most other "experts", but then again, I'm not just any other "expert." I'm a guy that's been at this longer than most of the other leaders in this game, and I've seen experts and students alike rise and fall (very quickly in some cases and very slowly in other cases).

If you start out by building a website, the next logical "trap" for you to fall into is the "must drive traffic" trap.

Building a website is probably step 4 or 5 at best if you are going to succeed online.

The first step is *always* finding your traffic source. That means finding where your target audience is *already* hanging out online and then strategically approaching the process of getting your ideas in front of that audience. This is why I love helping "newbies" start out with low hanging fruit opportunities like selling on eBay or Amazon. I know I can get you going in a successful direction on those platforms. The audience is there. A little training and a bit of creativity and you've got a $100K business *and* you are ready to expand into a website that makes money *day one*.

TESTIMONY: An example of building the website *last* . . . not *first*:

When I first met Nancy she was selling her handmade wreaths one at a time on eBay for a decent price, but after some coaching from my team and I, she grew her business to include informational materials teaching others how to build wreaths the way she did. She sold those on eBay as well successfully.

She also collected the email addresses of her prospects and buying customers on eBay and started to grow her mailing list. Once her loyal list was big enough she launched a website where her "fan base" could go to get more of what Nancy had to offer. (LadybugWreaths.net)

Her loyal following of "crafty" women now rely on her for the latest decorating and craft making tips and strategies. They even pay her for coaching and devour the content she produces.

She has the email addresses of hundreds of buying customers and many times more fans, and a very nice income as a result of her ongoing efforts.

Here's a great article with some fantastic feedback from my blog readers. We talk about building your *audience* before you build a website.

http://www.jimcockrum.com/blog/?p=308

The comments and "aha!" moments among the readers make it a priceless "must read" article.

5.5 "Driving Traffic"

"Driving Traffic" is a term I'm liking less and less all the time.

Most of the "how to" courses for Internet success will tell you to first "build a website" and then "drive traffic" or visitors to that website using any number of opportunistic strategies that will be entirely irrelevant within a few days, weeks or at best months after the "herd" starts using the same ideas.

Do you like the idea of being "driven" somewhere on the Internet? Would you like an invisible hand "driving" you where that invisible hand wants to push you? Do you like when your peaceful browsing experience is interrupted by someone "driving" you somewhere else?

Of course not.

> **HERE'S SOME INSIGHT:** *No one else likes to be "herded" or driven anywhere either.*

Contrast the term "driving traffic" with the idea of "attracting eager fans." Which sounds nicer? Which do you think is more effective? Which kind of business do you want? Which activity sounds like it has the potential for long term success?

The bottom line in "getting traffic" online is to create quality content that eager fans and partners are willing to share. Any other tactic or strategy or trick will be short lived if it ever works at all. I'll talk more about finding audiences and distributing your content in other places in the book. To be clear, you *do not* need a website to start this journey.

5.6 Virtually Everything "Step-By-Step" or "Push Button Simple"

If I've not made myself clear enough yet, let me emphasize one more time that anyone endorsing a "big launch," a "step by step" system, or anything "push button simple" deserves your *highest* level of scrutiny. Here's a popular blog post I wrote on the topic of "mega-launches" and Internet income products:

http://www.jimcockrum.com/blog/?p=259

In that article I set the bar *very high* for the experts who claim to be able to teach you something about making money online. Hold me, or anyone else to those lofty standards. Demand to see that there are numerous success stories. Demand to see that their customers all get to hang out together and discuss the ideas in depth. Demand to be allowed to wait a few weeks to get in on the "super deal." If the information is so incredible it will still be incredible (and available) a couple months after "launch" even though the guru claims it will be gone forever.

5.7 Eagerly Following Any "Celebrity" Guru

In the game of Internet business, big egos come with the territory.

Although I've met several very genuine and helpful people at the top of my industry, I can confidently report that they are all human, and as such they are all susceptible to the classic human flaws and none of them are 100% creative, innovative and helpful 100% of time.

All leaders are flawed. When it comes to teaching "how to make money" strategies you'll run into even more flaws among the leaders.

I think this is because it takes a special kind of humility to remain genuine and other-oriented once you are in the spotlight. Most "experts" fail miserably at this challenge.

Never become so enamored by a "big dog" that you check your brains at the door. This advice fully applies to me just as much as it does anyone else.

For example, I get emails occasionally from subscribers to my newsletter letting me know that they've dropped all other email subscriptions and will only be reading my Internet marketing email from now on.

That's just silliness.

There is no "one" guru or expert worthy of that sort of loyalty—I don't care who they are. Creativity demands that you be exposed to all sorts of ideas so that you can improve your filter and come up with great ideas of your own.

I rarely unsubscribe from anyone's email list. I read several every day and often times I learn something even from the blood-suckers in my industry.

But I'll *never* blindly follow anyone.

If you missed this blog post the first time I mentioned it, please go check it out now:

http://www.jimcockrum.com/blog/?p=944

Now I'd like to reveal the secret behind the pic at the start of this chapter!

This picture of my son and I was taken by my wife a couple of seconds before the picture that appears at the start of this chapter. The lesson: Don't be enamored by the results the experts are getting—make sure you know the full story of how they got there to begin with.

Concluding thoughts for Chapter 5

This chapter has been a reality check. It's been a slap in the face of some of your misconceptions, but ultimately I'm saving you a lot of heartache, *money*, *time* and pain. Trust me . . . I'm right on these things and have had no challengers ever prove me wrong or even attempt to.

If you feel like you've proven me wrong, or if you think I'm missing a valid point somewhere, *please* visit my blog and post your thoughts! You'll notice that I publish comments from both those who love me and those who don't. Agree or disagree—it's all a matter of public record and I love to kick around great ideas with thinking people!

Of course there are countless other potential scams that can be entirely avoided by doing some simple Google research before spending any of your hard earned money on any "slick" products. If the sales letter includes a yacht and pricey cars in the presentation or if it guarantees results or if it features someone trying to look or be "cool" as part of the sales pitch, then odds are it's going to have a 1% success rate or worse for the victims . . . I mean suckers . . . I mean customers who buy in. Many would-be online entrepreneurs actually buy system after system like this in search of the one idea that will work. I call this "shiny object syndrome." That's a condition that will destroy you before you even begin. In this chapter I've gone after the "not so obvious" dead ends, but there are plenty out there that common sense should tell you to avoid. You've been warned.

> **A CHALLENGE FOR YOU:** The next time you see a slick launch or big pitch for a training course or product that includes impressive statistics and "user results" be *very* critical, patient, and determined in researching the offer. Don't fall for the scarcity tactics (i.e. "only a few left at this price," etc.) Get the whole story and wait out the "big launch." If the program is good, it will almost

always be back again soon at a lower price anyway, or someone else will teach the same thing for a lower price. Stay focused.

CHAPTER 6

More Business Ideas

I've covered a lot of ground so far in this book, but keep in mind, I'm just one guy with my own experiences and observations. You very well may find a new and creative way to make money online that has nothing to do with what I've covered so far. If that happens, please contact me! We'll teach others your approach and help a lot of people if it's an idea that can be scaled out to others.

Please keep in mind as well that there are literally dozens of proven online income models that I endorse and have seen work for my students and clients, but this book is an overview of my favorites that I've seen work most consistently for the most people.

Below are some simple and highly effective business models that I've seen over the years that might inspire a new business idea for you.

- Selling vintage postcards, old magazines (or pics torn out of old magazines and books) on eBay

- Selling everything from cars to coins on consignment on eBay (consignment means selling for someone else and keeping a cut)

- Finding profitable inventory at storage auctions

- Writing books that can be pulled together quickly to sell on Amazon (using services like CreateSpace.com). Ghost writer sites like TextBroker.com can be used if you don't write well.

- Buying overstock, unneeded samples and other bulk inventory to sell on eBay or Amazon

- Buying used cell phones locally via classified ads to sell on eBay

- Using "retail arbitrage" to buy closeouts and "out of season" stock from any number of retail stores for high profits on eBay or Amazon

- Finding successful local small business owners in unusual niche markets and creating a "how to" video training series with them/for them to sell.

- Buying themed lego toys and holding them until the theme goes out of circulation and then selling them on eBay/Amazon

- A simple biz model of interviewing experts and creating content to attract prospects and grow an email list.

- Assisting small businesses by creating a simple smart phone friendly webpage for their business for a small fee. This often leads to a lot more consulting work for the expert for this single simple service.

For many more examples check out MySilentTeam.com—we have dozens of creative biz models to share there.

As my business has grown from these types of foundational activities, I've taken on bigger projects such as:

- *A best selling book*—101FreeMarketing.com (all proceeds are donated to an inner-city entrepreneur training ministry)

- Just as I was writing this chapter, I spent $2,400 on eBay inventory that *I fully expect my staff to sell over the next couple months for just under $10,000*. Once you know how to do it, it's easy to build a system and repeat your success. The system I'm using to find this liquidation inventory is taught as a course we call "LIT" training. I teach it along with one of my all time top students. For details on this biz model (with fantastic success stories) please visit this blog post: http://www.jimcockrum.com/blog/?p=2119

- *We manage two very successful membership websites each with thousands of paying members.* I launched these sites *after* finding my audience (I took my own advice from section 3.4 of this book—the part about "Finding Your Audience" first).

- *I also make a lot of money from affiliate marketing.* In fact, recently the largest product launch in Internet Marketing history occurred. I won't tell you the product that was sold (it wasn't mine), but I can tell you that of the thousands of affiliates promoting the multi-million dollar launch, I finished in the top

5 *on the planet* in total sales made. The product price tag was $3,000 and each affiliate got 50%. It was a great payday when I sold well over 100 customers this great product, but still . . . I *don't* suggest newbies start out trying to make money with affiliate marketing! It was the perfect product for my audience, it took a lot of work developing my readers to the point where they were ready for such a product, and I rarely endorse such high priced "launches" (maybe once per year if the product is *perfect*). Go back and read section 5.3 for my advice regarding affiliate marketing.

- We do *Consulting*. I also get paid to consult individuals and business on their approach to internet marketing and business.

- *I blog, make YouTube videos and write books* like this one to attract my ideal prospects and educate them on the concepts that will help them grow.

Concluding thoughts for Chapter 6

I now have over 50 people around the world who work either for or with me in some capacity, and we add dozens of new prospects and several new clients every day. I've built multiple systems without hiring a single employee. It's a fully transferable business as well which means all I need is Internet and I could live anywhere—but it all started out quite simply as you read at the start of this book.

The point is, you have to start small and build up gradually. If you persist, even a "small start" can be *very* profitable, and you have a lot of great ways to grow as you get your momentum.

If you are already started, aspire to grow and expand by automating and using the ideas, skills and tools I'm showing you. There are so many distractions that can waste your time—I'm trying to help you avoid those.

CHAPTER 7

Going Offline

Businesses around the world (online and offline businesses) need your help! ***Now!***

"Going offline" is one of the biggest business opportunities in the world, in my opinion. Right now as you are reading this chapter the demand for people who can apply simple, effective marketing strategies is growing and the supply of trained experts is lagging far behind. This is creating a *huge* opportunity for those of us who "get it."

I know this opportunity is huge because I see it everyday in my own business. I've had clients happily pay me $750 per hour or more in this opportunity. I've spent half a day with businesses that pay me very well, buy me lunch and surround me with VIP's to help them make the most basic of marketing decisions. I turn down clients constantly because they can't afford me . . . but if you are willing to take less than $750 per hour you can find plenty of work (and you *won't* be the one doing the "work" if you read this entire chapter).

This one trend is creating more success stories among online entrepreneurs than virtually any other concept to ever hit the Internet, and while this many sound like a sales pitch, I've got nothing to sell as I reveal the details of this opportunity. I'm just laying it out for you as best I can.

> **DO THIS:** On OfflineBiz.com we have over 12,000 active members all hanging out in our forums and discussing how to best assist each other and profit from this mega-trend! Stop in—many of the forums and resources are free on that site!

Here are the trends that are leading us towards this "offline bonanza":

- Traditional advertising methods are failing to get the results they once did for traditional businesses (TV, Radio, Newspaper, direct mail, billboards, Yellow Pages, etc. are all failing).

- More and more "offline businesses" (like restaurants, lawyers, tattoo artists, pet groomers, etc.) are waking up to the realization that "marketing" is no longer a matter of applying traditional strategies like I just listed above. They know they need to go online if they want to survive and grow.

- In most cases, websites that were built to help these businesses aren't generating any new business for the most part.

- Traditional businesses feel stuck and a bit confused by it all. They need help.

Enter the "offline marketer":

- You are the guy (or gal of course) who gets the phone ringing again.

- You are the guy who gets the leads coming in again for pennies instead of dollars per lead.

- You are the guy who makes marketing make sense again to traditional businesses.

Even if you don't feel technically capable of what I've just described you must trust me and go check out this website:

http://www.offlinebiz.com/

That site has 12,000 members (as I write this, it's growing!) spread out around the world as of this writing. All of them have one thing in common. They recognize the trends I just spelled out and they recognize that they can have an impact in this business opportunity without acquiring any new skills or technical abilities whatsoever.

I'll repeat that:

*Successfully helping "traditional offline businesses" **is not** a matter of applying your technical skills. It's a matter of **knowing** what works, and having a community in place (OfflineBiz.com) that supports your efforts when you have questions.*

The "hard work" can be done by someone else in all cases. You don't have to build websites, do any programming, or design any graphics. At OfflineBiz.com, we show you the simple online marketing strategies that work. Next we show you how to provide these services (worth thousands of dollars to businesses), while getting the work done by "outsourcers" or other low cost partners for a fraction of the value you charge your happy clients.

Read some of the success stories we've posted at OfflineBiz.com. You'll be blown away, I promise!

This business model (like every business model I ever expose my readers to) *can* be fully automated and outsourced so that it is nearly 100% hands free.

The OfflineBiz.com concept is my final and probably my largest "Silent Sales Machine."

> **TESTIMONY:** I've had websites since 1999, tried everything, never made a whole lot of money—$1000/month in profit was a good month.
>
> Since I started *this* business (OfflineBiz.com) about 2 years ago— I'm getting money and recognition and clients. I could support myself if anything ever happened to my husband (and that's very reassuring to me). I am getting a nice ego boost (and client boost) from a weekly newspaper column I've had for more than a year. I may have a new consulting client at hundreds of dollars per hour.

And *this* is in a "down" economy. I wonder sometimes what my business would be like if clients had more money to spend? I can think of few businesses I could have *started* in the last few years that would have paid off like this offline business model.

I also trust few people online as I do Andrew, Jim and some of the other folks I've met and worked with in the forums of OfflineBiz. This has been a life-changing resource for me. *Thank you*!

—Diana
  OfflineBiz.com member

TESTIMONY: I have found great guidance from <u>OfflineBiz.com</u> and really enjoy helping offline businesses get online. Offering marketing, websites, email campaign management and other services has been a great income stream for our family. I want to thank you for being there with this information, membership site and resources.

A client I picked up early on in my offline biz stream was our local Coldwell Banker Real Estate franchise. That one client turned into many as the broker is also the founding member of the largest law firm in our county and we picked up that side of the business too, along with several realtors.

What happened today takes the cake. I met with the Broker today to discuss some new marketing ideas I had and he stopped me in the middle of my speech to ask me a question.

He asked, "Instead of continuing this contract deal with you for marketing, how do you feel about coming on board with our company as a partner in the business and handling the online marketing just as you are doing now? The only difference, you will be earning 6% of overall income in the company as opposed to contracted income." This attorney/broker and I have found a real kinship in our business philosophies and values. He has grown to like me and wants my influence in the company weekly on a more consistent basis.

I didn't have to think long. This company, a new franchise in our area, projects 1.5 million in commission revenue this year, and that's a pretty payday at 6% even after company expenses. I am already earning about $1100 per month from this one client contact, but now will be earning significantly more with little extra effort than I give now. Although, I imagine after signing partnership agreements next week, I will certainly have a greater interest and likely spend more energy there.

I wanted to share this with you personally first, before posting to see if I can offer any testimonial for you on this as well. Liquidation, Offline Biz, and my small membership mailing list are all helping to make our dreams come true. You lit a fire under this frustrated entrepreneur, and I am grateful.

I realize this income may not be a fortune, or even compelling to some, but for us, it is a significant blessing and it's money being made in the real world with no hype or gimmicks. And from only one stream of income and only one client.

Thanks so much again, your provided resources have given us the tools we need to change our future. We won't forget it!

—B. Hamrick
   OfflineBiz.com member

TESTIMONY: I have been a member of OfflineBiz.com for over 5 years. I have been dabbling. This year I got serious and on my first sales call with an offline biz client I closed a $6000 deal to help him upload videos (video marketing) to YouTube and help him launch an eBay store. I am closing another client this week. Why did I wait!? If you can talk reasonably intelligently with people, you can close deals.

—K. Bunnell
   OfflineBiz member

Read many more success stories at OfflineBiz.com

CHAPTER 8

Where to Start

SO, What Do I Do Now?

Before I tell you what I think you should do, I want you to think about an amazing fact with me for a moment.

You and I are entrepreneurs (treps). Do you agree? Just in case you doubt it, consider this.

If you've read this book and if you are excited about the prospect of improving your life and the lives of your family members and the people in your community, your city & more by creating income streams that benefit you and others as you build legitimate income streams, then *yes it's true, you are an entrepreneur.*

Imagine . . .

Imagine that all of our fellow entrepreneurs since the beginning of time are represented by a pyramid. Most of them by design are at the bottom . . . and only a few are at the top.

I'll explain . . .

At the bottom of our pyramid (the widest part of the base) you'll find hundreds of millions of entrepreneurs who lived in the *impossible* times or in impossible situations in history. Maybe they were spending their days planting and harvesting or hunting for food just to survive and feed their families. Making a better life wasn't even an option. Still though . . . they had that unquenchable inner drive to create and improve processes and their own lives and the lives of people nearest to them. Sadly for most treps in history, it never was even a possibility. It could have been because of the heavy hand of their government, or the circumstances they lived under, the greedy king they served, or the "lower class people group" they were born into, but they realistically never had a chance.

As we move up a level on our pyramid we'll find slightly more fortunate treps, but still millions of *frustrated* entrepreneurs who suffer under even modern versions of anti-free market dictators and anti-business governments around the world. The red tape, risks, expenses and barriers to success in business frustrate nearly all efforts of these poor entrepreneurs. They have little chance. A few succeed and "escape" their circumstances, but the vast majority never do.

Just above the suffering *frustrated* entrepreneurs are the entrepreneurs stuck in the *hard times*. The hard times to me would be times like the Great Depression in the United States or the fifteen years after communism fell in Russia. Wars have created windows of "hard times" around the world. During these "hard times" it was possible to succeed in business, but you didn't have very good odds on your side. The common sense thing to do was to beg for a job or go somewhere else in the world if you could escape.

As we work our way up the pyramid we could add several other layers. At points in world history (and still in the most backwards parts of our world) being a woman or having the wrong skin tone or wrong religious faith presents huge barriers to any type of business success.

So, where are we now on the pyramid?

For the vast majority of entrepreneurs reading this book right now, none of the above mentioned challenges exist thanks to the freedoms we now enjoy and thanks primarily to the Internet which has created huge opportunities for all of us worldwide. We have a truly level playing field for the first time in human history with the most powerful tools ever made for treps at our disposal . . . for free or virtually free.

you are here...

"All Gizah Pyramids" by Ricardo Liberato

Pause for a moment and truly take that in.

There can be no argument that we live in the greatest time in the history of the world to be an entrepreneur. If you doubt that this is true, it's probably because you spent way too much money on a college education where they tried to convince you that we are worse off now than we were in the stone age.

Can skin color or religious faith keep you from selling on Amazon, building a mailing list or creating a membership website? Can your gender prevent you from putting up an item for sale on eBay? Does your government prevent people like you from recording interesting thoughts on your video camera and posting it online?

Seriously—what excuse do we have as entrepreneurs compared to our kindred spirits from virtually all of world history up until now?

The worst complaint I can come up with is *high taxes*. I overcome that by *making more money*.

So, what's next then?

The one asset you will have to develop if you are going to succeed is a good attitude.

- Complainers don't succeed.

- Quitters don't succeed.

- Victims don't succeed.

- Habitual tire kickers / refund seekers don't succeed.

- Magic button chasers don't succeed.

I'm not saying it takes an enormous commitment or even a great deal of focus to make many of these ideas work. I've seen some flat out *lazy* people do very well online.

We are at the top of the pyramid. Take advantage of it!

You actually have to *do something* though, to get the ball rolling.

THE FREEDOM OF THE "INTERNET LIFESTYLE":

Hi Jim,

I love your vision and what you've done to help so many people, including me! My wife and I have four young daughters, we homeschool, and my goal is to free my time to spend much more time raising my daughters, being involved in their schooling, and serving others together as a family.

As a family we spent seven years living in southern Mexico doing volunteer work, being supported by the donations of others, before returning to the U.S. almost two years ago. Since returning, I have been working to build businesses and we have really struggled to make ends meet, but thanks to you that is turning around.

At a breaking point about 9 months ago, I had the choice of getting a job (and watching a lot of my vision die), or immediately adding a significant new income stream. I chose the latter by investing in your JimCockrumCoaching.com program, and it was one of the best decisions I've made. It was worth every penny, as that training is now making me several thousand each month and allowing me to pay the bills.

Sincerely,
—C. Leake

That's one reason why Amazon and eBay have stayed so consistently at the top of my list of ways to get started online. Once you grasp the basics of either site, it's easy to move on to other bigger ideas. With eBay you can have a global business *overnight*. When else in human history was that possible?

Just in case you are mistakenly thinking that I'm one of those "gifted" or talented exceptions to the rule, check this out:

Here's what my excuse list would look like if I wanted one:

- I have no idea how to build a website.

- I'm not a good writer (thank you editors).

- I got B's and C's in high school.

- I had a C+ average in college.

- I hated marketing class in high school and college and got bad grades in it.

- My parents are both alcoholics (clean and sober since I was 10, but still . . . it's a rough start!)

- I got fired from my last real job.

- I have 5 kids to feed and my wife doesn't make any income.

- I'm not well-connected in my local community.

- I hate getting up early.

- I don't like to learn new skills (nothing technical, please!)

- I really don't like to work at night or early in the morning.

- I'm quickly bored by anything routine.

- I don't consider myself a good writer—it doesn't come easily

- I'm an introvert

- I don't like being on camera

- I'm easily distracted and move on to new projects . . .

. . . are you getting bored with my excuses yet? I could go on if you want me to! Those are all 100% *true*, but they aren't *complaints*. Those are the parameters I work within and still succeed with relative ease. I pull in high six figures online working 15-20 hours per week with no employees. I have various partners around the world working for me and with me.

Better yet, I've been a part of teaching literally thousands of other people to overcome their excuses and succeed online as well.

Are you next? I truly hope so!

Where do you start? What are the steps to success online?

There's not "one path" that you can take to succeed online. Your gifts, skills, attention span, personality, drive, experiences, location, connections, interests, availability, creativity and yes, having a bit of cash to invest are all factors in which opportunities are available to you.

All that being said . . . *I do teach people to succeed online no matter where they are starting out!* I have fantastic coaching, courses, free newsletters, best selling books, thousand of successful students willing to help you out, free blog posts, YouTube videos to share with you, and over a decade of success with all of it.

A couple of important factors are *time* and *money*.

Do you have *time* or *money*? Most people have one or the other.

If you have both, you can take your time and soak in the ideas of this book or my free newsletter or membership sites slowly.

If you have neither time nor money, I'm *sure* that the section of this book about Amazon.com and eBay.com are the best bet for you as a starting point.

If you have a little money to invest in your business, I suggest you try the ProvenAmazonCourse.com course, or if you are a bit more serious of a student who is ready for coaching and ready to invest in what I *know* is the best coaching team on the planet, then call us at the number below. Our success rate is off the charts. We'll work with you until you succeed.

1.800.994.1792

The chart that I showed at the start of Chapter 4 is a great place to start as well.

There are numerous fantastic business possibilities online, but following the crowd *will not* get you there. Following one "celebrity" expert **will not** get you there. Following *any* high priced big launch "step-by-step" programs *will not* get you there. Read Chapter 5 again before choosing a path.

Rest assured though—I meet and hang out with people *every day* that have made great things happen online, and there's no reason you can't join us.

CHAPTER 9

How I Earned $112,500 in 3 Minutes

Do the math. $7500 x 15 = ?

How did it happen? It's a simple story that took a bit of time to develop, but I think you'll like the story. If by chance you skipped ahead to this chapter, I'm hoping this chapter will convince you to back up and read the rest of this book!

If you recall, I showed you this picture earlier in the book back in Chapter 1:

That's a picture of the first live event I ever hosted. We had planned on around 50 people showing up, but we wound up filling the room and turning off registration at 350.

There weren't any professional speakers or big ticket items sold from stage. We broke all the rules of "holding a successful Internet business conference."

What we did worked though and it illustrates nicely how differently I do things in my organization.

The feedback we got from the attendees was incredible. The event was 100% content and success-story driven. The ideas presented on stage all weekend were based entirely on the ideas you've just read in this book.

We brought every day "real people" to the stage all weekend long and shared creative "Silent Sales Machine" stories with the audience . . . one after the other after another . . . all weekend. You could have heard a pin drop much of the time. Tears were shed, lifetime friendships were established . . . it was incredible. It wasn't about me one bit . . . it was about *ideas* and *real people* with great stories of success.

> **DO THIS:** To read more about this event visit this link:
>
> http://www.mysilentteam.com/public/CES-1-Conference-Videos-Learn-Why-So-Many-People-Said-This-Was-The-Best-Conference-of-Its-Kind.cfm

So where does the $112,500 come into the story?

After a weekend of sharing my best ideas and various success stories from guests, I made a simple 3 minute offer to the audience.

I told them, "I'm taking 15 attendees (only 15) and for $7500 you will be a part of a small group that meets with me twice in the coming year. We'll get together, have some fun and help grow each other's businesses."

That's it. It took less than 3 minutes actually (you can hear the entire sales pitch in the video of the event).

We got over 20 applications. I picked my favorite 15, and we ran with it.

I'll bet you are expecting a sales pitch at this point, right?

Sorry—no sales pitch. I don't work that closely with strangers. You *are not* being invited to join my small group.

The fact is, all 15 of the people we accepted into the group were people I not only *knew*, but *knew well*. They were all having a degree of significant success and had long ago read this book and taken action based on the ideas in this book.

In other words, I knew each of the 15 were serious, trustworthy, dedicated and positioned for success. Building that kind of relationship takes time, energy, commitment and integrity. Those are the sort of people I work with.

I send the "fast dollar" seekers elsewhere . . . I have nothing to offer them.

You might be asking why I wrote this final chapter.

There are a few reasons. I hope . . .

- You are more likely to believe that the ideas I'm teaching in this book really do work. **Credibility.**

- This chapter makes you understand that there's nothing *easy* about success online, but if you follow a proven system the sky is the limit. **Realistic enthusiasm.**

- You feel encouraged by the audience of fellow readers who you can see are taking this book very seriously as the foundation for their online adventure. We hang out online together and spur each other on. Join us! **Community.**

- You buy into my "slow and steady wins the race" philosophy of online success. **Strategy.**

"Wealth gained hastily will dwindle, but whoever gathers little by little will increase it." —Proverbs 13:11

—Jim Cockrum
JimCockrum.com

Use Facebook?

We have a large community of online entrepreneurs and fans of this book who hang out online together—I hope you'll join us! Here's the link:

https://www.facebook.com/groups/mysilentteam/

Are you interested in working with one of our coaches one-on-one?

All of our coaches are students and readers who started out reading the book you are now reading and went on to succeed online. Once we noticed their success, they were invited to coach with us. I fully believe we offer the best business coaching experience that the Internet has to offer. Get more details here:

JimCockrumCoaching.com

Have you got the latest version of this book?

Things change all the time, but I'm committed to updating, improving and passing this book out to past customers for free.

Get the latest version of this book on this page:

www.mysilentteam.com/public/720.cfm

18063518R00117

Made in the USA
San Bernardino, CA
27 December 2014